American
Idiots

Mr. Jack Doyle

ISBN: 147528232X
ISBN 13: 9781475282320

Dedication

Dedicated to my father John F. Doyle who served his country in the United States customs with honesty, originality and integrity for thirty-eight years.

He taught me how to love my family, my country and to speak truth to power and to seek improvement in all problems encountered in the many venues of life.

Also to my wife Phyllis for her patience, understanding and proofreading.

AMERICAN IDIOTS

Ask What You've Done To Your Country

1. BEGINNING THE POLITICAL JOURNEY   1

Politicians and the Capitol   - N.J. politics

Ike Eisenhower, The ONLY GREAT REPUBLICAN IN THE TWENTIETH CENTURY

OBAMACARE, ROMNEYCARE PERFECT TOGETHER. 230 years of futility.

THE DUMBOCRATS-party symbol a jackass!

INTERJECTION; THE FARMERS OF THE CONSTITUTION

Letters to Senators McCain and Obama

Why Me? The TWIN TOWERS and Pentagon

SLAVERY CONSTITUTIONAL, LINCOLN RUINED THE SOUTH AND THEY VOTE REPUBLICAN.

2. NIXON AND FORD   45

"I am not a crook   "But he was a crock!

Ford in Nixon's future

"Well, Pardon me" landed him in Saddle River, NJ instead of Up the River, NICE DIGS !

Two shifty cities in Ocean County,NJ-lessons unlearned

3. REAGAN RON UP THE DEFICIT -A LAFFER !   59

Doing the Voodoo tax cuts,Daddy Bush applauds After All

What Ailes us is very Foxy. Thanks to a Patriot Newt's Sex Drive
The Question is Newt

Atomic Man! Cost of Nuke Arsenal.

THE REAGAN MYTH-Congressional Record

FOX NEWS IS THE ENAMA

4. CONTRACT ON AMERICA   69

The REAGAN DEPRESSION unemployment AND VOLCKER

Believe it or not A FOUR YEAR BALANCED BUDGET-not for long

Banking Revisions – Gramm's building blocks for Dungeon of Debt

GRAMM CRACKERS-Mom and Pop   UNIVERSAL MEDICAL CARE-
FALSEHOODS and Deceit SUPREMES AND THE CONSTIPATION OF
THE U.S. (U.s S.uckers)

THE REPUBLICAN CLOWNGRESS AND ETCHASKETCH CANDIDATES

THE SUPREMES AND THE CONSTIPATION

GLOCK MEMENTO IN BUSH LIBRARY

A LIGHTBULB GOES ON-FREEDUMB

5. THE POISONOUS BUSHES   159

Daddy made me Presidunce ! "W" ACTION FIGURE IN FLIGHT SUIT.
NOTHIN ACCOMPLISHED

Shotgun VP, "Deficits Don't Matter" Torture to read!

For bush library -Never ending nor paid for wars without plan

For bush library- Never ending Tax Cuts and Deficits

"Grovel" Norquist leads GOP INTO Dungeon of Debt

NRA TERORRFIED - ltr to Cong. Peter King

New State JUSTICE-PROVE YOU'RE PHOTOGENIC AND WHITE TO
VOTE

MESSY REPUBLICANS, nationwide.

Romney Mansion w/2 Car Garage

SUPREMES ARE CATHOLIC IN DECISIONS

6. OBAMA'S 2012 ELECTION NECCESARY TO SURVIVE 237

OBAMACARE/ROMNEYCARE KINDA LIKE THE SAME?

UNIVERSAL MEDICAL CARE -FALSEHOODS and Deceit included.

THE CONSTIPATION OF THE UNITED STATES

CORPULENT CHRISTIE CUTS MEAT from NJ Budget

FAT REMAINS - SAVES 101 YR OLD TUNNEL

ALLOW ME TO DIGRESS

CONSERVATIVES SPEAK IN TIME

HE MADDOF WITH 50 BILLION - the one percenters

COX NO COP

GROVEL NUTTWIST

ASK WHAT YOU HAVE DONE TO YOUR COUNTRY - HOW COULD YOU BE SO WRONG?

A 75 YEAR EXAMINATION AND OBSERVATION ON THE RUINATION OF A NATION THAT MAY SOON CEASE TO EXIST- THE REPUBLICAN PRESIDENTIAL PROCESSIONAL ROAD TO RUIN - DR.FEELGOOD REAGAN THROUGH THE POISONOUS BUSH AND HOW AMERICANS LET IT HAPPEN, -.AND NOW THE FINAL CURTAIN?

Authored by a man who voted for Ike, Goldwater, Nixon and Reagan (once).

Okay, maybe you feel it wasn't your fault, after all Ron Reagan had Nancy the bobby soxer of 65 so cute!

And John Wayne liked him and so did Frank. He used to be a registered Democrat and changed .What better recommendation?

And his kids didn't like him just like in every family with a busy rich Dad. And he had Roger Ailes and a bunch of other PR types from Hollyhoodwink to cover up the few flaws so folks really thought he said "Gosh Mom, I forgot to duck" heroic! And the public thinks he fought deficits while really increasing American debt over 500% without a war in eight years, a mere detail and not his fault. Must have been Democrats , tax and spenders that they are. An underground cell.?

So after Ron and the CIA spook Daddy Bush 4 year term we were six Trillion in the debt after the "inept" Carter left us with only a half billion deficit ,Ron and the Republicans made the number Trillion worth understanding. Really, did anyone know? And did Reagan really raise taxes eleven times? I don't believe it !

PLEASE follow the sickening story and hope we can get out of this American tragic fiasco created by people who vote and the propaganda masters of American politics . Even they didn't know the Frankenstein monstrosity they were creating until it was too late.

FOREWORD:

TO THE READER ;   As a first time writer I apologize for any lack of organization but this book is not "ghostwritten" since I have no publicly famous name and have had an education as well as considerable experience in American business and politics .I did not feel my vocabulary was lacking and I could express my thoughts and feelings clearly without assistance.

If Grandma Moses could paint at an advanced age I could write, though my typing is awful. I see Rodney King authored a book recently in spite of the terrible beating the LA police gave him so I commend him for the thoughts he put forth at this late date .Just as an aside I recommend the police not do that again, seems it created a stir. Then again a better more astute judge and jury might have prevented the subsequent problem. Rodney in my opinion is and was a gentle soul undeserving of such treatment.

In this book you will find some letters I sent to various individuals and government officials thrown in as I saw they fit. Hope you find them interesting.. they were for cumulative effect rather than instantly attaining their purpose. A reply was not expected since Congress persons and President Obama are busy.

Senator Bill Bradley was a running mate of mine in Denville,NJ many years ago when we both won our election, my elected post was Councilman and to me it was a big deal and we shared a fine local citizen ,Anthony Iannacone as campaign manager. We spent time planning strategy and analyzing our efforts and the competition we faced and made some public appearances together including one with Danny Thomas' daughter .Bill's new book "We Can All Do Better" was just published and I commend it to you.

Bill certainly did better than me.

In my opinion his prescriptions to "do better"will be difficult to follow considering the attitude and filibuster tactics of the R party especially if the newly elected Indiana primary winner'statement about his intention to be "more partisan" as a Senator if elected is any indication of the future in the GOP brainless mindset. What sweethearts.

Another recently authored new commentary, "It's Worse Than It looks" by Norman Ornstein and Thomas Mann ,two gentlemen astute and perceiving nails one of the major faults of the current media on the ass with the critique ``In our past writings we have criticized both parties ...Today however, we have no choice but to acknowledge the core of the problems lies with the Republican party....It is ideologically extreme; scornful of compromise; unmoved by conventional understanding of facts, evidence and science ;and dismissive of the legitimacy of its political opposition."Further, "We understand the values of main stream journalists including the effort to report both sides of a story. But a balanced treatment of an unbalanced phenomenon distorts reality."

My book KNOWS THIS AS FACT and incorporates such an approach, I'm sorry they put it so well in advance of my effort but congratulations sirs. Also your skewering of "Noogie "Norquist whose mystifying hold on robotic Republicans is unknown to possibly 90% of American voters is helpful in EXPOSING the influence of`` Dollarpower" on the GOP and how their tax policies for the wealthy buy elections and ultimately bring OVERWHELMING deficits.

Much of this book can be termed a RANT but why the hell not?.Three years effort and appreciable money to publish entitles me .It would be satisfying if some of the people we write about were in jail. You should feel the same. And finally, my family loves me.!

PREFACE-THE FINDING OF TRUTH IS NO LONGER DIFFICULT

With the advent of Google anyone who spends a THIRTY minute session at the computer can discover almost all they need to know about a subject, at least enough to lead them to a better understanding of the facts about almost anything and everyone There are thousands of leads to follow and referrals that will tell the truth if only one wants to know it. The more time spent the more facts are available to everyone quickly without traveling to the far corners of the earth or the universe with no need for a University education.

Knowledge of the keyboard on a word processor is important but 20 years of higher education is not necessary. Ability to read and use a dictionary is essential .

The understanding of semantics is also important.

With this statement I am telling you the reader why there are no bibliographies in this book . This is not meant to be a reference guide but a wake up call to you to follow your conscience in leading a life that can benefit you ,your family and mankind if only you put your knowledge, your fortune and efforts in elections and political arenas to the best use for the good all Americans.(remember them?)

Not just you!

Speaking about important movements and political happenings with knowledge is also a contribution every citizen can make while living a meaningful life.

I am confident that what is printed on these pages is true. I have no political affiliation that is sacred to me, no religious leaning of any kind that would benefit me in any way. What I have written is only for the good of this country and to lead the reader to the path that is necessary for the survival of the United States and MAYBE the world as well. If it angers you so be it. To show the purity of my intentions;

A personal litmus test EXAMPLE, when JFK wanted to cut taxes back in the early part of his death curtailed administration I felt it better for the country to continue building the US Treasury with taxes despite my salary of $110 per week with a wife and child in my mortgaged home. Lyndon Johnson finally got the tax cut passed later. And now look! Where'd it go?

There is nothing in the extreme written here - just observations that can be proven by the test of time and results in the past ,..many of them SAD BUT TRUE..

I am hoping for your sake, "You can't handle the truth" as spoken in the movie is

NOT SO!

INTRODUCTION

So you know, dear reader, where I'm coming from. I was a true Depression baby and have always had a foreboding impending sense of doom.

One of my first recollections is hearing the banker who held the mortgage on our first house announce to my parents that foreclosure was in three days, and my mother crying.

A budding avenger and hero, I told my mother I would "get them for that" --- I was six years old (maybe seven).

We rented that house in Bellevile,NJ for about three years but then my father found a much nicer area to move to that was a short walk to a beach. Surrounded by lakes so almost as in the movie "A Wonderful Life," we, like Jimmy Stewart, survived and prospered because dad come up in the ranks as a government employee and was able to purchase our 2 bedroom 1 bath home and pay it off in five years.

Franklin Roosevelt was the only president I knew in my growing years and my father hated him - railed about him at the dinner table at least three or four times a week but America was solvent much to the benefit of millions, including my dad.

Many years later, after a achieving a degree in government, I came to realize that desperate times call for desperate measures and FDR, his ideas and those of the men around him, were a life- saving application to a nation dying with an unimaginative, unyielding Federal Reserve Board , stultifying policies and an unimaginative Republican party, which fought every progressive program including Social Security until the end of the Second World War.

Upon FDR's death, Truman stepped into the presidency and the decision to use the atomic bomb made the end of the war blessedly hastened with millions of Allied casualties and Japanese as well avoided as well as the massive expense of invading a country 7000 miles away from our heartland and industry.

America for various reasons has never found it expedient to use atomic power again, although Eisenhower threatened it to bring North Korea to the table and Clinton used the same threat against the same country at one point.

Sad to say, Afghanistan would have been the perfect spot for the use of such power and technology: it had been a cancer on the world for decades in the 1900's and the harboring of Bin Laden and the Taliban government would have been sufficient to justify a well placed bomb destroy-ing those responsible for September 11th and preventing the disastrous course we have followed since that time with ill-chosen World War Two tactics.

This author was dismayed , disgusted and nauseated in finding the people in charge of our defense over decades allowed this nation to spend over twelve Trillion dollars on atomic weapons never to be used or even contemplated for attack.. This expense was and is crippling and useless and now renders us helpless financially in every aspect of nationhood. Why didn't some whistleblower stop them?

It is nauseating to think that dynamite, invented in the U.S. during the 1800's, can be holding America at bay in two theaters of war. This DuPont invention is killing thousands of our troops and costing us trillions that we cannot now nor ever afford.

Returning to past history and the thread of my story if the reader cares to fathom it. . .

World War Two, being the last war American really "won" if you can win any war, brought forth great achievements by our armed forces and civilians alike. Women flocked to the defense industry as men went to war and after 1944, many mothers stayed in the work force, many by choice. In that era, a decent paying job supported a family without both parents employed. This did not continue, as we have seen. They were the good old days.

CHAPTER 1

WHAT I AM OR WHAT AM I -YOU ARE AN AMERICAN OR ENGLISHMAN, CANADIAN, ETC. BY ACCIDENT OF BIRTH, \ NOTHING IS INGRAINED IN YOU BY THE GEOGRAPHICAL LOCATION OF YOUR BIRTH.

Many of us are Catholic, Methodist,, Episcopalian, possibly Jewish at adulthood because of our parents drilled it into us rather than any conscious choice made in growing up .It should be pointed out there are 3200 recognized religions in the United States. ,many nuances of the same themes and others are totally different in thrust.

Unfortunately there are only two major political parties in America and too many citizens are stuck in a rut because of their upbringing by parents who injected their politics and religion into their offspring.

In many cases these parents had never been outside of a 500 mile radius from where they live, they read little of any background of the broad world outside and certainly have no knowledge of how their voting choices determined the success of the country and indeed the world. Not to be snobbish but these are the Red States,read "Red State,Blue State"

All too many times we hear "I am a Democrat" or "Republican" simply because too many people never studied history or read more than one newspaper during a lifetime and that one a local shopper / obituary /wedding/graduation tabloid and a weekly at that. Many listen to a drug addict as their only source of "news" or watch Fox "news" as it is based in unreality.

Growing up believing one`` IS ' ANYTHING POLITICALLY IS IDIOTIC.

Many ,especially foreigners never graduated from high school and bore a child, which restricted their ability to travel, learn or broaden their outlook by schooling.

These people are limited to what they learn from sound bites on TV or the Limbaugh show on radio or from what they hear from their peers at work or the local food store ,hardware ,tobacco ,grain store ,tavern or church .

They are referred to as "Sheeple" for good reason. They "follow" one info source.

Sadly it is the manipulation of these people by political parties that determines the future of this nation. Too often this has resulted in calamity for the United States as a whole.

As the the Nazi party in Germany flourished on the Big Lie under Propagandist Joseph Goebbels so did the Republican Party when Ronald Reagan brought image makers and paid public relations experts to Washington DC..followed later by Carl Rove and minions..

The head of FOX news ,Roger Aisles a high echelon Reagan operative was enlisted by Rupert Murdoch after the "R party lost out in the Dole election fiasco so he could spread biased accounts of everything that happened affecting political opinion thru the Fox TVand radio networks as well as his newspapers throughout the US.

Rupert Murdoch has a William Randolph Hearst desire to control the world through his media with a Neanderthal right wing slant that can ruin all but the wealthy while still placating what is left of the middle class. The latter will settle for sports, a six pack(not stomach muscles) pretzels and chips, crosswords , gossip columns and half truths for news. TV reports are skims of 3minutes not worth viewing for facts or conclusions.

The Obama arrival in politics of a brilliant young mixed(mutt by his own description) race candidate who enlisted many other brilliant young crafters of opinion thru the internet has taken away much of the power of newspapers to radicalize the American scene as well as the strength and middle of the road approach of CBS,NBC and ABC although sometimes they can be "had" on certain issues. If all of America watched and took to heart the message of the Fox media the R party would have won again in 2008.

But there was no hiding from the voters the devastation left by Bush which negated strongly against the GOP.

But the right is not giving up and they are strongly defending their disastrous journey into the hell of depressing recession ,10% unemployment, money center bankruptcy and never ending trillions dollar wars 7000 miles away from our heartland and supply centers and deficits to be paid by our great grandchildren.

Since their defeat at the polls in Nov. 2008 The R party has paid political "advisers" fresh from the Young Republican clubs in wealthy colleges to appear on talk shows, they are pretty young women or handsome men to speak before chambers of 'Commerce and to write learned tomes on

"CONSERVATISM AND THE FUTURE OF SAME" as if it had really existed in the past 3 decades .They do this with corporate donations.

Remember Reagan took us from 500 billion in deficit (total after 200 years) to THREE TRILLION IN EIGHT YEARS without a war!

And today ex Cabinet members of the bush era appearing on TV talk Sundays full of disdain for new ideas even if those ideas are approved by polls.

One Bush press secretary had the audacity to state that attacking Iraq was the RIGHT thing to do so they would not attack us again! AGAIN ? Huh,what history book.?

EX VP Cheney stated that taking over Iraq has prevented them from developing 'MORE WEAPONS OF MASS DESTRUCTION" MORE?

Remember bush on TV looking under his desk for these figments?

As if there had ever been any. ! (just so you know even bush admitted there were none)

This is the communist method of re writing history with the Nazi style big lie upon lie upon lie hoping that eventually some of it sticks in the ear of the over easy uninformed.

But hope springs eternal in the cold hearts of the R party because they are convinced they are RIGHT and that they can con the American people into the feeling that everything the new president and his cabinet enacts will be wrong(and there's a good chance some of it will be in view of the numerous inherited messes-remember the 800 billion bailout sprang from the bush treasury secretary and with no oversight) And the checks sent out to all tax payers were just enough to pay for higher gasoline prices paid by all drivers for the prevous year meaning "no stimulus," resulted ,just catch up.

JACK DOYLE, author, grew up in a town where there was little to call attention to the area except as a vacation spot where "city people" from NYC suburbs had small second homes for use only a few months a year. In the 1930's anyone with more than one home was considered well off or " rich."

Merchants and townspeople controlled the sleepy governing body with four to five councilmen including a mayor selected by them and from them each year. Usually they named the man who had the most "pull" in some fashion and he would repeat for several years without opposition since the town almost always selected a Republican slate with no opposition from Democrats. The County was similarly inclined with no operating two party system for years and a nomination to Freeholder insured four years of a SMALL salaried position for the winner with a second term usually guaranteed as long as the incumbent avoided rape ,burglary or embezzlement charges.

But there was and is plenty of rape of County coffers during that period under the table or in hidden corners making some men who earn a modest income into well heeled public figures Before the 1960's there were no investigative reporters looking into sources of officials wealth and the local newspapers weeklies heavily dependent on the printing of township notices for income and therefore township officials.

An example later from a different county but nevertheless indicative of what went undetected

Township officials usually had a means of under the table remuneration in some form by shaping local laws that benefited property they owned in valuation or preparing them for paid postions elsewhere after they had served the town with no apparent conflict of interest.That's why they "served" at little or no salary and ostensibly they were "dedicated public servants" in the minds of the voters.

As World War II ended more people from the cities migrated into the area as full time citizens or their children moved to town .They remodeled or enlarged their summer homes and commuted a distance to their places of business via the DL&W RR or Lakeland Bus and the voting pattern showed a glimmer of two party government with the budding occasional Democratic party bringing competition electing an inspired vocal minority representative to the township board. Over decades some towns with a preponderance of "city folk" turned Democrat. But not many.

Even with this the area, Morris County, remained a heavily(60% or higher) Republican leaning population though many who live there are working people with modest means and no wealth in their backgrounds. It is a testimonial to the lasting power of the Eisenhower sweep of the country and the brainwashing that the R party has instilled in the county from one generation to the next.

Doctor Feelgood Ronald Reagan,the great dissembler carried the party flag forward and was like a second shot of Republican enthusiasm.In this county.

Independent thinking is scorned and ridiculed by schoolchildren as well as adults.

This is what I refer to as THE STEPFORD REPUBLICAN SYNDROME

It is no coincidence that the words clones and clowns are similar.

This aura or mindset is a template for the Red State - Blue State breakdown that now afflicts the United States of Ignorance .(my term)

Despite a selection of widely circulated publications most of us, the broad American public reads no daily newpaper and in many suburbs there is only one which may be slanted by one political point of view. The use of the public library except for an occasional student is a rarity and therefore there is little awareness in the broad sweep of small town USA . In financially troubled times as we have now caring citizens do use the library instead of buying the newpaper.

Political "commentators " such as Limbaugh, O' Reilley and their ilk have taken over as founts of "information" for a broad spectrum of the American public and in middle America towns where there is little airtime for opposing views their word is gospel .This in spite of one being addicted and the other a sex phone deviate.

The largest share of Americans still think Iraq was responsible in some part for the bombing of the World Trade Center despite the fact that even those who made that claim, the Republican Administration has recanted it as has Joker W Bush who looked under his desk in a TV skit for "weapons of mass destruction".while US soldiers died because of his Con job and his NEOCONS.

.The largest percentage of Americans believe that our National Debt is less than ten trillion dollars and have no idea that the social security fund is being raided to pay for interest on the debt ,the war in Iraq and massive tax cuts effected in the first years of the baby bush administration..

But I digress .Let us examine the Eisenhower administration's good and bad points.

1 TO THE READER.............

Events and facts presented in this book are filtered through my intellect which has been honed since birth (1932) by 75 years of life in the United States. This includes four years of study for an AB degree in both Government and Psychology at Drew University in New Jersey, and several years of Law School in the same state.

I served in Europe as an enlisted man in the occupation forces prior to the signing of the Second World War treaty with Germany in theMedical Corp. My American wife joined me overseas and we had our first child Debbie born in Frankfurt. Upon discharge during fifty two years in various businesses I was involved initially in what was the largest pencil company in the world and then proceeded to outside marketing responsibility in the same firm traveling in most of the United States and once in Europe .Along the way I was an owner of a retail establishment in Central Jersey. My involvement in and deep interest in politics will be outlined later.In this ,my first effort at authorship there is no effort at favoritism for any political party , philosophy, or creed.

My first vote for US president was cast twice for Dwight Eisenhower , then Richard Nixon ,afterward the landslide loser Barry Goldwater. I had a photograph signed and

inscribed to my family by George Bush because of a donation to him in his primary effort against Ronald Reagan
.When it came to the election I capitulated and voted for
Reagan,only that time... I was regretful afterwards.He was a
false leader with PR.

The largest donation I ever made to a presidential candidate up to now was to John McCain in his primary
effort against w. bush (deliberately uncapitalized).
Had McCain won the Republican nomination that
year the ENTIRE WORLD AND AMERICA would have
been so much better off than presently there is no
imagining.. Mac knew war,the cost and the futility of
same.

His change to supporting the Iraq war when bush ran for
his second term was self seeking the next presidential
nomination because Jeb Bush wouldn't run., due to
the fact that Jebs kids were drug addicts,a plague
that seems to have infested Republican families.

Afghanistan would have been a onetime war and there
would have been no invasion of Iraq and terrible consequences that have spewed into American culture.

As to religion after a highly consuming interest and some
research into several between the ages of 14 to 19 I
developed and maintain to this day a great skepticism for all. I attended a Methodist University where
almost half of the undergrads were prepping for the
ministry. We never agreed.

From my standpoint "I am a camera" politically. Choosing
one political party , the Democrats in 2008 was surely
a necessity based on facts if this nation was to sur-
vive considering the clown show on the road for the

Republican presidency in 2012 and the Republican brand of lies, hypocritical greed and mendacity.

My bibliography for this book is;

All Public Libraries,Newspaper,magazines

Google

Life as it presents itself today and always: .

Look around you.

THE UNTIED DEMOCRATIC PARTY OF THE UNTIED STATES OF AMERICA

Whenever an important measure comes before the Dumbocratic party is seems to be a skunk at a lawn party within days after it is offered. Splinter groups form almost at once like a THIRD WORLD COUNTRY with tribes and clans.

Every individual Dem seems to have to prove he is " independent and thoughtful" not bound by any measure of loyalty to a leader of party but only to his own values and "voters who elected him".This is the glaring weakness of the " Dums ", they can go their separate ways so many times they become an unparty.

The R party loves this and in spite of the fact that the solid R vote in Congress can defeat an even larger majority in that "august body" on so many important issues the Dums continue to act like cats that can't be herded.

As witness only recently Mayor Booker of Newark, N.J. a black Obama so called supporter who stabbed his party in the back on a Sunday TV show after playing football games with Corpulent Christie, Republican Governor on a TV commercial. Thanks Bro!

Mark Twain said "I'm not a member of any organized political party,I'm a Democrat"

Republicans love this and rely on it in their strategies and it harms the population of the USA.

This is the Democrats ' perpetual pattern for disaster and glaring weakness as a group that cannot be trusted to bring about important changes in a system that desperately needs change.

Why is the filibuster still possible after the Dumbs had 2 years a full 60 votes in the Senate and votes in the house to end it? And there are other ways even now such as threatened by Senator Frist in his term as Senate leader.

Sen. FRIST came from a billionaire group and family that owned a nationwide profitable healthcare firm. His main purpose was to prevent anything like OBAMACARE OR ROMNEYCARE happening in America. He left elective office and government serving one term before accomplishing that . Obviously he felt the Supreme Court would do that for his firm as it is a CORPORATION.

IKE (DWIGHT) D. EISENHOWER

Dwight Eisenhower was the first president the author voted for in 1954.His candidacy was a subject I chose to report on in my senior year at Drew University under the greatly respected Professor Robert Smith who passed away only recently in his nineties.

Basically I studied the newspapers, periodicals and magazines of the time and predicted which states Ike would win in the election after winning the primary with almost no effort.

Eisenhower won all but one State, this writer predicted he would lose two. That's how popular this war hero was and deservedly so. There was no hint of arrogance in his demeanor despite his wonderful history and impeccable background as commander of the Allies invasion and victory in Europe.

Ike was not a politician or even an executive statesman but an honest person who gave his best to the country during the eight years he was president and the only hint of self aggrandizement was his acceptance of the Gettysburg farm embellishments (Ike bought the farm before his entry into politics}by members of the oil industry which in character he donated to the US government at the end of his term.*

Because of the proximity to Washington D.C. Gettysburg has become a weekend Whitehouse for all presidents that followed, a working weekend / vacation spot benefiting our country's subsequent presidents and becoming part of American history.

During his term there were many evidences of favoritism to the oil industry in general but to be fair the Congress also leaned heavily toward oil company supplication by lobbyists.

With a Republican President and Congress laws and governmental decisions leaned toward all industries.

Despite this Eisenhower warned against the corrupting influences of the military and industry in his famous speech at the end of eight years in office.

Eisenhower was criticized by Ronald Reagan for this very prophetic and timely warning since he was a willing "taker" of gifts during his time in office .The co star to a chimp in Hollywood had an affinity for donations by those who supported him and whose bidding he did as president.

Ronald Reagan's acceptance of a home on the cliffs of California tax free from industrial magnates of the Fortune 500 in the year after his term in office was arguably the most egregious Ex Post Facto bribe of all time .Because it was from conservatives no one bitched! If Dems had been involved Congress would have held months of hearings.

But I digress so more on Reagan later in another chapter.

*The smaller Gettysburg farm was owned by Ike prior to his entry into politics but it's size and scope were greatly enhanced by Cities Service Oil Company by gifts given privately and quietly during his years in office.

Strangely prior to Ike's departure when Nixon was nominated for the next President when asked by news reporters what Richard Nixon,hisVP had done praiseworthy during his term Ike said,'" Give me a week, I'll think of something."Later his son married Julie Nixon, daughter of Richard and Pat.

Nixon LOST THE ELECTION.. The glow of Eisenhower's EIGHT YEARS OF ASSOCIATION did not carry enough impact against Jack Kennedy charm for the Republicans since Nixon had the five o clock shadow debate and an unhappy past in California campaigning to live down as well as a scandal about bribery in his past that was exploited by the Democrats.

Nixon's comeback supporting theVietnam war devastated Democrats who felt JFK was close to ending that disaster when he was assassinated. Another instance of GOP war-whores at work. MIC !

I will never forget seeing film of Marble Mouth Sec.of State KISSINGER and Nixon telling the head of Saudi Arabia to raise OIL prices so he could afford to buy a fleet of American made fighter jetplanes they needed like a hole in the head to protect their nation against ISRAEL as if we would ever allow that! Especially in that era .

Obama didn't do that.

GOING WRONG, -GOING BROKE

The Republican road to ruin from Reagan to Bush . What about Nixon?

The Republicans have conducted politics recently as if it were an "all in" poker game or an internet version of "HITMAN" .No Doubt this is because they are at the end of their game as far as impact on the Whitehouse or Congress using conventional tactics such as advancing good ideas thru legislation and consideration during Congressional sessions and subsequent votes or having sit down meetings with the Democratic party seeking compromises on important issues.

NEW IDEAS have been replaced by NO IDEAS. The party of NO. Congress stand still.

They grew used to having complete control of all functions of the government during their disastrous eight years in office when deliberately fomented false fear induced voters to support them in all manners of costly wars and mismanagement .The second installation of Bush as a "war" president broke America in mind and heart.

.Near Bankruptcy has been the result .

The folly of having a system that permits sons of previous presidents to run for office and appointees to the Supreme Court take over the job of Presidential selection when they are placed in the job by the very relative who has every interest in seeing his progeny win is a massive fraud forced upon America by the weakness of self interested law.

And when that same person, George Bush can take upon himself the duties of selecting stocks and financial tasks of a massive Wall Street Fund while his son makes decisions that will enrich that fund we are all screwed.

And that's what happened in 2001-2002 when Poppa Bush was a key stockholder of the Carlyle fund and sonny boy was president.

Naturally the ability of the elected people in Congress to trade privately in stocks and bonds while members of Congress made   fortunes for many of them who had no qualms about their good fortune due to inside knowledge.

Much of this has finally been put aside in March of 2012 with new federal laws against such politically advantageous manipulating due to a ''SIXTY MINUTES" TV expose that revealed and embarrassed many Democrats and Republicans involved.

MY HOMETOWN-THE STEPFORD GOP ENCLAVE

Where I live in Ocean County,N.J. there are more than an estimated 65% Republican voters, 25% Democrats

And ten percent of the residents do not vote or have an opinion as to which party should govern the USA or even the town in which we live. Most Dems remain silent .Not I.

This is plain in viewing the district voting records the day after an election published in the local newspapers that still cling to publishing.

Many of the residents of this golfing - gated active senior community think the United States has won the war in Iraq .They believe the false Petraeus "victory"creed.

What brings this to mind is the opinion of a quite vociferous supporter of georgie porgie w.bush . My community is a Stepford Republican enclave most of whom would have kept bush for another term and this guy's attitude is a perfect example.

Publicly and openly this man thinks we have won the Iraq fiasco despite daily reports from that country of anywhere from 1 to 80 or even 100 Iraqis being blown to bits while living their daily lives in buses, marketplaces, places of worship and roadways.

The same goes for his obliviousness to reports of dead American soldiers, one at a time or several, this to him is the price of winning even though their name, rank and hometown are in the news every day.

The existence of 740,00 Iraqi widows and even more orphans living on American support in tents must seem to him part of the victory.

Never mind it is our deficit printed money that keeps them alive now and for the foreseeable future.

What is more aggravating to me and anyone who has an idea of what a win is(Germany and Japan one week after the capitulation in each theater WW2) is that there will never be a "win" because we of attacked the wrong country . Victory was already in the hands of Bin Laden and his theory, co opted from Karl Marx that his ideas and organization "will force the capitalist countries to spend themselves into destruction' which as of the day after the Republican win of the White House in 2004 was already baked in the cake ..Little w. bush's policies for the future ruinous four years in Iraq and Washington,DC assured this.

There is a constant sickening drumbeat about our having "won'" the War in Iraq.--- orchestrated by a cadre of R strategists who see their futures sinking . Pamphleteers at the

NRC send out weekly talking points to keep their dwindling base of faithful working and hoping(and praying, let's not forget the Christian right) that Republican candidates in the next election will have the right to say Obama was wrong and admitted we won the war by the "surge" Because he praised the troops during his visit there.

.They will also pray that when we remove troops in great number from this disastrous area there will not be inter-necine wars and a "bloodbath " in spite of the fact our presence there has caused an invasion by Al Quaida that led to the deaths of Americans and the unwitting Muslims of the country that became an accidental war theater .

A blond bimbo ageing "young Republican" on TV stated today that Obama was talking about how he was elected to end the war in Iraq and she was hurt that he was not declaring an intention of "WINNING THE WAR".

Look at the facts and admit dear heart that there is no definition of a win there because no one in charge had a plan that was thought out and now if we had the way it would be too late. The camel has gone out from the tent. This writer had early conviction of this a long time ago in 2003 when the armories and munition depots in Iraq were raided and stripped of weapons and ammunition by rebels while Rummy Rumsfeld stated simply "Boys will be boys" putting out the naïve explanation that the populace had been held down by Hussein too long and that the weapons would give these raiders a sense of being able to defend themselves and their homes!

Since hand grenades, bombs and machine guns were in the arsenal the statement was asinine.

During the same time museums were stripped of 170,000 art pieces from thousands of years ago that were apparently known to collectors and ordered "on theft" like tickets for dry cleaning or a fish store purchase..

That week I knew the so called Iraqi Freedom war was lost as we could not provide even the basics of peace keeping in a country already riven with religious strife and obliterated infrastructure .And besides we were neglecting Afghanistan to make "The Decider" and his oil mafia look good.

ANOTHER DAY OLDER $76 TRILLION IN DEBT

This 80 year old author was born in Newark, NJ with a debt of 34 cents and now look!

EACH AND EVERY citizen of the United States is born with a debt of $ 260,000. growing daily which increases due to more spending to keep afloat and interest compounded. It's lucky interest rates are below 1%.Who did this to me and you and our kids, READ ON !

Born in the Depression year of 1932 the author held high paying jobs in corporations and in my own wholesale business in states from Mass.to Florida.

Read how THE REPUBLICAN PARTY and its' misleaders of the past 50 years

LED AMERICA INTO RUIN .

We'll see if America can get out from under and how. Who will lead us to a path of survival and solvency and when?

Newspapers and magazines at this writing were asking in the past few years whether the GOP needs a broader party or a purer one. Nationally disgraced individuals like the previous Vice President Chump Cheney are publicly embracing wonderfully "effective and necessary " tactics like torture in a variety of forms to the world and American citizens . And if you have a brain in your head you might ask why is this party still in existence?

The Republican ex VP has an approval rating of about 12% and the former President bush about 26%., a used car with that value off list would be scrapped .

If the USA needs a second party, HOW ABOUT A SOCIALIST PARTY ? (The happiest most secure nations are socialist)

Or perhaps a party headed up by Arnold Schwartznegger A SEX WITH THE HELP PARTY?

A KEG PARTY? (COULD BE LED BY MANY MEMBERS OF THE

SENATE OR HOUSE)

A CONSERVATIVE PARTY EXCEPT WHO CAN QUALIFY AS CONSERVATIVE AND WHAT IS IT.? Is it Republican, are you kidding? Look at the tag team of bloviators on the podium at the "Presidential debates"in October 2011 each one trying to outdo the other with schemes that a twelve year old high school student would not agree to if he valued his future.

This, because they are trying to appeal to their base "base."

Neanderthals ?

PRESIDENT REAGAN IS WIDELY TOUTED AS A CONSERVATIVE BUT PLEASE WHY?

IT'S LUDICROUS AND RIDICULOUS.HIS EIGHT YEAR DEFICIT INCREASED BY 300% OR MORE WITH NO WAR TO PAY FOR. And he got a free pass for the Savings and Loan disaster costing over a Trillion dollars "off budget" What the hell does that mean? It didn't go away!

Ron Reagan Jr. has stated his father had Alzheimers while in office. Administration executive publicly and bravely protect citizens against decisions made by a mentally incapacitated chief executive?

See what Reagan's budget director David Stockman has written about his administration and the resulting deficits. "We're simply deferring massive taxes unfairly and immorally putting huge debt burdens on future generations and that is just wrong." REAGAN MYTH . . . The Progressive Review

prorev.com/reagan.htm

Reagan conducted one of the most absurd **invasions** of **American** history, targeting the tiny Island, GRANADA. which covered up for ... Reagan's previous decision to send troops to **Lebanon that cost** 241 Marine lives AND RESULTED IN AN EVACUATION only thirty days later which he said resulted in a more "defensible position" It truly was a defeat but Granada was a PR move that changed the headlines that focused on Labanon.(ALSO COST DEAD SOLDIERS) Of course Stockman is late to the condemnation after having taken part in the rape of our previously semi workable economic system. Perhaps better late than never but no Reagan idolizer wants the truth.

PLEASE   NOTE" --
----------------------THE REAGAN ERA WAS THE START OF"CLASS WARFARE" that Speaker of the House of Reprehensibles ,Boehner, says Obama is inspiring! WHAT a sick joke, between Reagan and Bush the1% at the top of the wealth tree have had a real increase of 300% in purchasing power and the MUDDLED CLASS stagnated left with chicken feed and fish food over a thirty year period.

Some estimates are more stark and can be proven at 400% compared to 45% considering higher proportionate costs of medical insurance and deductions for FICA for lower income workers.This inequality is the cause of lower standards of living and spendable income for the vast majority of the purchasing public and THE CURRENT MESS IN AMERICA and all over the world .

And PaulRyan Republicans believe that cutting Americans' medical care, retirement benefits and food stamps will cure the malady they created. They are the sick ones with a superb medical and retirement plan .The 99% pay for that. So, "Occupy Congress."!

As this was written the State of Minnesota had only one Senator even though five months after the election in November 2008. This is because the Republican party clings to the belief that all's fair in love, war ,and politics. They continued to finance appeals and recounts of the number of votes in spite of the fact that same recounts have resulted in even more voters who favored the Democrat and the Republican incumbent has been defeated.

Nationally we also see the spectacle of Republicans holding "Tea Parties" in high dudgeon about taxation that has been changed and threatens to change more in favor of workers who earn a living and not the super rich of top 2% favored in the Bush tax cuts of the past 8 years. These posturing are ridiculous on the face of it , modestly attended publicly from what can be seen on TV and in the few newspapers that print photos about them but the mere fact that things are slipping away quickly from the previously controlling GOP is what makes these hypocritical scenes even more disgusting.

They can't stand what is happening all around them and to really point out how stupid the whole thing is. Governor Perry of Texas threatens to secede Texas from the Union. (Perry is later known as "Whoops") This of course borders on madness and would be legally and fiscally impossible. But that's Texas thinking for ya!

The fact is are there were more funds spent on wars that are were not winnable at their outset and more taxes not levied for the costs incurred than ever in history. In the previous 8 years our national deficit thanks to bush more than doubled.

The costs of Wars are off the books ,a brilliant accounting move by, you guessed it, Republicans! the total cost of wars in Iraq, Afghanistan and Pakistan to the U.S. Treasury and ignores more imposing costs yet to come, according to a study released on Wednesday.

The final bill will run at least $3.7 trillion and could reach as high as $4.4 trillion, according to the research project "Costs of War" by Brown University's Watson Institute for International Studies. (www.costsofwar.org)

In the 10 years since U.S. troops went into Afghanistan to root out the al Qaeda leaders behind the September 11, 2001, attacks, spending on the conflicts totaled $2.3 trillion to $2.7 trillion.

Iraq and Afghanistan are now in their 10th years and threaten to be longer yet ,more than triple the time it took to win The Second World War which is really the last war this country truly "won" .If you disagree please explain what a win is in your mind.

The USA now is in the position that the GOP minority rich placed it in and the Obama administration must spend money to stimulate the economy as guns ,hand grenades and ammo do not stimulate a local economy for civilians. .the national economy is failing because of the depression forced by the defilers and pillagers who are doing their best to make present Democratic plans "fail" as the once heavily drug addicted commentator Rush Limbaugh prefers .

It is heartening to see that the man who wrote the book "Rush Limbaugh is a BIG FAT LIAR' is now the citizen's choice for Senator in Minnesota. HOORAY.!

Please DO read this book, it puts this incomprehensibly popular right wing loudmouth under the microscope and in the proper light. If one wonders why the title is so deliberately insulting you will know once the contents are digested.

Then it is obvious

The author prior to his Senate victory, with a great sense of humor of course ,has great insight into the truth about the man he wrote about and politics and government as well. By the way many folks are jokingly hoping that Texas will be able to secede and take the W. Bush family along to be president and take the planned library with them.

Sept. 6, 2008

Senator Barack Obama
713 Hart Senate Bldg.
Washington,D.C. 20510

To Senators Obama and Biden

I am offering a plan that would benefit the entire country and particularly the auto industry about which McCain says"those jobs will never come back".

Back in the Reagan years there was some semblance of control on foreign car imports but he was soft on those controls for which he was rewarded with a million dollar payment after he left office for a one hour speech in Japan; quotas disappeared during the deficit building Reagan years.

It is now time to save our industry and at the same time the country by reinstating a quota amounting to at least 15% less than what was shipped in to the US by all foreign nations from 2005 to 2008.

Foreign countries Germany and Japan and Korea must be reminded of what we have suffered because of them and done on their behalf in the past century. We must explain this is a case of survival for our nation where every sovereign nation must participate in making us solvent once more over the next half century. Our 58 Trillion dollar debt and our 320 million citizens ,

95% of whom dropped in standard of living over the past 8 years demand this.

From a standpoint of macro economics our debt equals the entire net worth of individuals and all industries in the country. These are incontrovertible facts .The United States can be Bankrupt in ten years if no special plans are enacted.

The auto quota can be adjusted over the years but it will hold down crime in areas where large unemployment has resulted in " alley survival " and help states that are incurring multi million dollar deficits in social safety net plans .

The auto manufacturer would have to do their part in guarantees of certain systems,drive train, engine, electronics and the like such as some Japanese German and Swedish makers in each car for at least 50,000 miles and 4 years.This could be worked out in advance with auto industry heads and truly should be improved on.

If there are recriminations from foreign nations we must remember other than underfunded Communist China we are the largest single consumer market in the world and basically we are needed by every nation as a customer. - .Also that our largest export product group is low profit or no profit grains and scrap metal that create few jobs.Our other export has been jobs as you well know.

The "flat earth" exponents have not suffered lost income, bankruptcy, lost medical care, lost houses to foreclosure and loss of net value of 30% in their homes I am sure. It is time to take them to a reality check with the former Comptroller of the Treasury who I believe resigned in disgust.

This plan can be expanded to other industries with some imagination and I would welcome the chance to talk with you both and work with you to assist America in a Democratic inspired survival plan prior to or after election. It is desperately needed.

Jack Doyle

Senator John McCain

Washington,DC

Dear John,,

My wife and I supported you with a fair amount of donation about seven years ago when you ran against George W. Bullshit.,THE INEPT OIL BABY.

You have now gone with him in so many ways it has made you into a near clone.

You say the Al Qaeda will follow us home if we don't stay with the surge crap. Do they all have passports or perhaps some of them are the illegals you and Teddy are trying to legalize .Or perhaps they can teach themselves to swim? Or MAKE THEIR Toyota trucks AMPHIBEANS?

Remember how many guys died and came home walking dung heaps forever from Korea and Vietnam? If we had stayed there how many more dead? Perhaps we could have signed a trade treaty with Vietnam at better terms for them if we have let them kill more of us? We lost in Lebanon and Mogadishu as well.

Tell the electorate what good we are doing overseas with a handful of cannon fodder on extended tours(what a screw job) against one billion muslims who hate us.

After we leave they will still sell us oil just as Hussein did after we beat him with the coalition forces even though we bombed his cities into dust. They will still need customers.

You and the other nine candidates all looked like pups whipped by GWB last night. I' am sure the Military industrialist supporters will love you all.

You are not a patriot if you don't agree with all of the above , just a wannabe dictator like Dummy Dubya. REMEMBER THERE ARE WAY MORE OF US .

Jack Doyle

The Best defense is a good offense was never truer than in the context of warfare.. It is essential to understand the essence of the Muslim extremist thrust which is to either convert all those people who do not believe as they do or failing conversion to kill them. This explains their desire to totally destroy Israel and the Jewish religion.

Unfortunately America has chosen to believe in the Christian doctrine of forgiving and turning the other cheek, bargaining and cajoling, threatening ,boycotting and a host of other ineffective actions when confronted with foreign intrusions of any sort.

Let's contemplate what it cost us to allow a group of " religious students" to seize our embassy in Iran back in Carter's single term as an ineffectual intelligent president.

Also what it has cost us to allow Afghanistan to harbor Bin Laden after 9/11 and our reliance on the movement of forces from here in The United States to a country with no roads or government to remove the Taliban from power (if only for a short time.) and the ensuing debacle of the insurgency of bearded sandeled tribesmen armed with Uzis and IED's

In the first case Jimmy Carter decided to try without success to rescue the embassy staff with inappropriate equipment and a heroic doomed Captain America effort. He completely ignored the internationally known fact that when an embassy is taken over by another nation that is an act of WAR If the offended nation does not declare war on the other that is the start of a massive defeat on the international scene de facto.

OPEC be damned, they needed us as customers and in a score of other ways and the dropping of appropriately reduced power Atomic bombs in Iran would have held off any thought by later Muslim extremist s(including Bin laden)

of attacks on the United States in any form for fear of total retaliatory destruction.

The same holds true in the case of Afghanistan.

A well placed atomic weapon in the area of Bin Laden's group in Afghanistan would have prevented the following;

Our invasion of Iraq at a cost of thousands of American lives, the earned enmity and contempt of one and a half billion Muslims who now have no fear of us and the resulting complete bankruptcy of our capitalistic banking system.

The loss of our wars in Iraq and Afghanistan. *

The collapse of the world economy because we undertook more than any nation could afford under the leadership of a neuter completely unsuited for his position..

The plan of Bin Laden was clear and is more obvious today. He can justifiably feel he has won a jihad against the United States.

Please recall when the Communist Manifesto by

Karl Marx stated"We will force the capitalist nations to spend themselves into destruction "

Bin Laden adopted this same concept (SIC) "When we send out two warriors to unfurl a banner showing Al Quada you Americans spend 100 million dollars dispatching 10,000 Marines to that area something we will force you to do time and again until you have exhausted your wealth."

So read the newspapers, look at the TV and Google the internet and learn how this has become a reality. .

*As of March 2009 we are sending 17,000 more troops to Afghanistan and probably more later. Our Generals state flatly we have not won the war and in Iraq we still have over 300,000 Americans in harms way ,truck drivers and "Diplomat

Guards " costing upwards to $400,000 each per year and news article dumbly point out that insurgent attacks have "diminished" to 100 per week.Oh, only a hundred?

As of March . 2009 -Casualties - 240 dead Iraqis per month and a few dozen American soldiers And this is an "improvement" ? NOTE; Thousands of tribal Insurgents (sunnis) have been paid to stop killing American or coalition forces and at this writing Iraq is taking over the cost of making these payments with a dwindling budget because of the drop in oil prices.

.There are upwards to 100,000 recipients of these bribes set up by Gen Petreaus

You may well ask what would have happened if we had employed Atomic Weaponry in the middle east so please observe how the Japanese occupations by the Allied US forces went and how our relations with the now peaceful country have gone since Hiroshima and Nagasaki.

This writer was an occupation troop in German after WW 2 and lived with the Germans and other American troops with wives off post in an apartment built from the rubble of bombed out ruins.. There was no insurgence because defeat was self evident and we had the Marshall plan which helped Europe including Germany rebuild under intelligent supervision and their own plans. Businesses thrived and Americans were welcome and"liked"

Now compare!

ALLOW ME TO DIGRESS

As Of Three Days Ago, Rodney King passed away, REALLY sad because he could have enjoyed the results of his literary pursuits at this stage of life. Surely the beating he took had nothing to do with his death?

It has occurred to me to doubt my ability to transform my thoughts into understandable literature or more important

–interesting reading and then I recall the chore of reading "Catcher in the Rye" by Salinger and worse yet "the Brother Karamazov" by Dostoyevsky who seemed to forget what he named his characters on previous pages or even chapters. Ol "Dost" seemed to take diabolical pleasure in giving four or five names to the boys in his tome.

And it was so sad and dragging ..

As far as the "Catcher" I knew more interesting characters than those drawn in the automobile trips from the thirties depicted in that book and my 1939 Cadillac burning a half quart of oil and 6 gallons of gas per mile would have told more exciting and interesting tales. And don't ask me about Chaucer, Shelley and Keats PUHLEASE.!

And why didn't Shakespeare write in American? These authors were required reading so that's why we all know them!

Now I return to the main theme of my literary effort by naming A FEW OF MANY Republicans who sadly are always in the news who are flat out bastards, there are worse terms but I leave it to the NJ Senate president to employ them. As Casey said you"could look it up"

One is Super Gov. Corpulent Christie of NJ who at present is trying to make another attempt at Vice President out of a tax cut in a state that is sliding off a deficit chasm. Vote me in ,I cut taxes is the typical Republican entreaty from desperation gulch in lovely downtown Trenton.(and everywhere)

Governor Christie, serial liar who has publicly been called the sexual appendage (censored) by others ,has cost the people of NJ billions of dollars in a short 18 months in office and has doomed commuters and NYC job seeker to a single underground tube 100 years old for the foreseeable future. All while dropping the ball on a half billion dollars in school aid from the federal govt. and lying about it blaming and firing his educational commissioner, a FORMER FRIEND. The damage to Education in NJ towns is massive and continuing. He has proposed a ten percent income tax cut favoring the richest while the state is broke and owes billions. And the NJ pension fund is 10 years in arrears.His plan to borrow money to finance a deficit is outright SICK considering how broke our grandkids in NJ are already. Christie in his PR efforts refers to the present state of the state as a comeback "by reformers" ,EEEEGH GADS !

Then unfortunately there is Mitch McConnell who truly resembles (take a look) a well dressed turtle.. Mac's major claim to intelligent governing by the minority leader of the US Senate has been to proclaim the "most important thing that we can do is to make Obama a one term president" apparently forgetting the need to replace the many million jobs lost by his party, the need to safely withdraw from the TWO TEN YEAR LOST WARS ,the Trillions in taxes given away to the rich kids and supportive corporations,and a host of other subjects . Of course his comment will sound good around the old spitoon at the feed store back home.

Then there is Sen Jim Dimwit of South Carolina who is a Pee Party" leader" and the intellectual of that group .During an interview on MSNBC on July 6th pronounced that there was no need for additional income for the US Treasury and that reduction in spending was the answer to balancing the deficit. Stated tax income for the past several years was in excess of previous years A visit to the Politifacts Truthometer will show how this buffoon gets by on the ignorance of his listeners or constituents. Recently he asked Jamie Dimond whose too big to nearly fail bank JPMorgan lost in excess of three billion dollars THROUGH "CLEVER DEALING" for financial advise for the US Treasury, AND in a fawning way as well.

And going back in time, honorable mention to William F. Buckley of the posturing intellect with big words everyone would look up. He "got off" on a tax EVASION charge in Republican controlled tax court. I briefly encountered him as he sailed his yacht in Connecticut waters from empty slip to empty slip to avoid docking fees. My friend with a sailing yacht with a fireplace told me this piece of gossip as we bid Buckley farewell motoring away from one slip to another in the same marina one foggy day. At that point he had not yet faced the tax court so he had to save on Yachting costs!. Buckley formed the stodgy " National Review "`` to read Dwight Eisenhower out of the conservative movement",we can see how successful he was . – it caters to the nearly dead rich folk of the US.

Typical conservatives , all the same, hypocritical and openly artificial except in their own eyes.AND JEB BUSH DOESN'T LIKE THEM EITHER!

FACTS AND DEFICITS MEAN NOTHING ! FDR and OBAMA are responsible.!

TWO HUNDRED THIRTY SOME YEARS OF FUTILITY IN AMERICAN HEALTH CARE .

On March 23, 2010, the Patient Protection and Affordable Care Act (PPACA) became law, providing for major changes in health insurance.[19]

AS of April 2012 with 26 Republican legislatively control-led states complaining to the United States conservatively controlled Supreme Court that the Obama sponsored and Congressionally passed PPACA is unconstitutional it appears it will be determined as such in whole or part. The major complaint is the government should not be able to require citizens to buy health insurance.

The contradiction here in my opinion is the government is allowed to force citizens to go to war against people they do not know ,fight and die against them even if the individual likes the group he is forced to do mortal combat with.

Further along the same lines all States in America have been permitted to require automobile insurance for purchase of a vehicle AND THE RIGHT TO DRIVE IT. and this is constitutional . By extension everyone requires medical care at birth and in the course of life can be forced to call for it during an accident in the home or highway at great cost that should not have to be absorbed by others as in todays' insurance configuration. Serious sicknesses on life's path costing hundreds of thousands of dollars befall people of modest or no means and this must be paid .

All Americans during the early days of this nation's formation were required to purchase a firearm so that all citizens were prepared to participate in a militia if needed and this was ordained by Congress and signed by the President. These facts are precedent.

Lest the Supreme Court jesters and members of the 9% approval rated Clowngress feel we do not need to change our healthcare system we should look at rapidly deteriorating physical and economic facts in America in 2012.

Regretably Life expectancy at birth in the USA is 50th in the world, below most developed nations and some developing nations. It is below the average life expectancy for the European Union.[11][12] The World Health Organization (WHO), in 2000, ranked the U.S. health care system as the highest in cost, first in responsiveness, 37th in overall performance, and 72nd by overall level of health (among 191 member nations included in the study).[13]

[14] The Commonwealth Fund ranked the United States last in the quality of health care among similar countries,[15] and notes U.S. care costs the most.[16]

The USA is the only wealthy, industrialized nation that does not ensure that all citizens have coverage (i.e., some kind of private or public health insurance).[17] In 2004, the Institute of Medicine report observed "lack of health insurance causes roughly 18,000 unnecessary deaths every year in the United States."[17] while a 2009 Harvard study estimated that 44,800 excess deaths occurred annually due to lack of health insurance.[18]

On March 23, 2010, the Patient Protection and Affordable Care Act (PPACA) became law, providing for major changes in health insurance.[19]

THE AARP IS FULLY IN FAVOR OF THIS PROGRAM AND SARAH PALIN IS NOT.

DOES THAT TELL YA SOMETHING? IT'S JUST LIKE THE ROMNEYCARE PLAN IN MASS.BUT DON'TASK HIM ABOUT IT,HE MAY FIRE YOU. ARE YOU LEGAL?

THE SUBJECT OF SLAVES. Author's note ; I felt this subject important so moved it to the beginning of this treatise on America's problems.

The darker skinned residents of the United States before and after 1776 were considered chattel by law and constitutionally. They were bound to their owner and they contributed greatly to the wealth of the colonies and then the United States, mostly in the Southern portions of America but to all of the thirteen original states.

The White House was built by black skinned slaves.(Finally they have been given a bonus kind of)

This was considered a philosophical oversight on the part of supposedly Christian beings at the time, a theory foisted on us after the civil war when guilt was not assigned to the "founding fathers" but the origin of rewriting of history began.

Rewriting history has become an international political practice for every nation and government.

More recently we look back at Communism and Russia, China and the George H.W. bush regime in the United States. (W for Witless or War Whore) And Reagan re write fans a la 1984 and Aldous Huxley.

Returning to the Constitution it is and has become an icon of cultural lag in the past 100 years as witness the slavery issue.

Teaparty icon Michell Bakcward stated the founding authors of the Constitution were strongly against slavery and made every effort to prevent it despite the fact it was institutionalized in the Constitution and existed in cruel form over 100 years.

Abe Lincoln changed history and culture in the United States freeing black people from slavery and was probably the last Republican president who really helped the entire black race with the sweeping federal change.

At this writing a learned Senator from one of the most backward states in the Union has said regarding a female Hispanic nominee to the Supreme Court (more on the "Supremes"later) that a few statements made 8 years ago (paraphrasing) seem to indicate that her feelings as an Hispanic and Woman would sway and bias her decision in one direction. History of the many interpretations of the constitution since it was established seem to indicate that feelings and backgrounds of the nine sitting justices do all of time render a personalized decision one way or another. This is why most decisions are not unanimous .

The fact that there are a preponderance of justices on the "Supremes" appointed by Republican presidents would seem to bear out my last statement on the question of gun ownership.

The most recent decision seems to indicate that the "second amendment militia" clause enables a gun to every person and when we see the National Rifle Association favors Republicans in support with large sums of money it is not surprising. But it is a sadly twisted interpretation especially since the term "militia" refers back to an entity having no existence in states in modern times. Again an example of cultural lag.

Any true construction semantically of the second amendment implies and demands a restricted right to bear arms only by those in a strictly organized government "militia" which in the era of farmers was required to protect the civilization of a town ,city, county or state in the absence of federal troops. In the 16th Century that was a necessity for law and order.

That five robed robbers of logic , law and order,peace and tranquility could pass such a judgment as the one sent down from the SUPREMES on the guns for everyone and anyone ruling without snickering up their black sleeves is unimaginable.

Check out the mandatory reports on contributions by the NRA and confirm this.

Meanwhile tens of thousands of innocent civilians are killed and families are destroyed by guns available like candy from a vending machine while other civilized countries have such incidents in lesser numbers by 60 to 80 percent because they control gun sales and possession.

This error of outlandish proportions continues to tear at the fabric of inner city and rural life alike with children shooting multiple numbers of their classmates to death with family weapons and gangs killing bystanders and drug couriers alike with no concern with collateral damage.

What was really handed down to us is really a Constipation.

The Rogues Gallery of Republicans of the 20th Century and beyond.

These are the leaders who led America wrong starting with; Ronald Reagan (See the Myth of later section)

Reagan took office when the US was only 500 Billion in debt and left the American People with a 3Trillion dollar debt incurred without the expense a war of any kind.

America has been paying interest on this debt since Reagan left office.

He further burdened future generations and governments with a tax plan that had no way of ever paying back this massive debt in spite of proponents of the Laffer Curve .Truly a joke that is a laugher. Laffing past the graveyard . We went broke building A bombs(see later).

An actuary can tell you how much this left as a permanent and burgeoning debt for the American people and how it left the rich far richer and the middle muddled class and working classes far poorer.

Reagan and his cohorts partnered with Democrat Senator Bill Bradley as a co sponsor of this tax "reform." Both Reagan and Bradley personally made millions by this reform.

I voted for Reagan..and ran on the same ticket as a Dem with Bradley.

I was disappointed and voted against Reagan the second term.

Of course not all Dems are innocent as we will point out and they can be tools of the political game as they are twisted into shape by circumstances and "compromise" in the flexing and flux of the Democratic system.

After all the promise of a tax cut to any segment of the voting public on the part of candidates usually and particularly Republican candidates is very hard to argue against during the ebb and flow of an election campaign. Today it bites in the Ass.

The promise of pie in the sky is hard to resist in the voting booth.

This can be seen even now with the United States in the midst of a debt exceeding multiples of the entire gross income of the country and no possibility of stemming the increase due to the mounting interest owed to both American institutions and foreign as well including sovereign Communist countries.

Nevertheless we see speeches from Republican candidates for every post from municipal,, County and Statewide positions for a REDUCTION of the flow of income to a governing body in spite of budgets that have holes large enough to foretell disaster in the near future.

New Jersey with 25% poverty as of 2012, California, South Carolina and other states are examples which I will not bore the reader with. Agreements made by previous governors ,legislatures and public initiatives with no thought to future costs have placed entire populations on the brink of fiscal ruin and dependence on a bankrupt national treasury to bail them out. California is on the brink because of a childish tax revolt years ago.

AS Crazy Eddie of TV Store fame used to SHOUT in his ads, "THIS IS INSANE"

THE TREASURY DEPARTMENT COMMUNIST AND THE SENATOR

Senator Everett Dirksen called my Father a communist on the floor of the Senate

Some time during the 1940's because my Dad was an executive of the National Customs Service Association and as such his assignment included calling on members of Congress during that period when the estimable Senator and other Republicans were pushing hard to appear frugal .You know how that is. One of Dirksen and others' aims was cutting border guards to reduce the national budget. The Association of course brought evidence this was not a good idea and the dispute reached the newspapers.

My Father had warned a Congressional committee publicly that drug smugglers as well as illegals would quickly take advantage of the cuts .He also wondered aloud to newspaper reporters if Dirksen would call him a communist when not protected by the rule of Senate immunity. That never happened.

As a result of John Doyle's effort compromise was reached .The original effort to cut 800 Border Patrol was reduced to 400 with promises to increase patrol agents in later years, -the following year 200 were added back as I recall and. of course many more guards were added over the years but just like locking the cockpit doors on airplanes to prevent hijackings -"too late!" And never enough.

Recently National Guardsmen with orders to stand down have been assigned to the border which has done nothing. .As I write this NJ National Guardmen are loading for Iraq which seems sure not to help in Texas, California, Arizona or any border state.

Iraqi police are quitting to join the Mahdi Army.,mortar shells are falling on Green Zone(safe area?) embassy personnel and Americans are dying. Iraqnam I call it. But back to the past.-

The US Government built a large office building in D.C at a cost in excess of 200 Million dollars, it memorialized Senator Dirksen (a strong supporter of the losing Vietnam conflict) ,it was dedicated in 1955.

Meanwhile the cost of drug smuggling to the US since that time along with illegal immigrants medical care, welfare and education for illegals has climbed over the stratospheric figure of a Trillion dollars which does not show up as a cost in our federal budget since much of it is paid by the States, Texas, California, Arizona, New Mexico and other alien targeted states where Americans lose jobs to undocumented illegals .

As the Senator is reputed to have said, "A billion here,a Billion there " etc.

My Father went on to become President of the NCSA,and after having worked in US Customs for decades retired for 30 years and passed away at 96. He is interred in Passaic ,N.J, with a simple in ground plaque shared with my Mom. In my opinon he is further memorialized by MONUMENTAL STUPIDITY on the part of the government he served for over 38 years.

And these policies continue at record pace.

WHY ME? ANBODY ELSE READ OR THINK AHEAD JUST A LITTLE BIT?

When the Boeing 747 airliner flew into the World Trade Center I watched as the smoke billowed from the 68th floor of the first building hit. I thought and hoped against hope it would be a small plane that was piloted by someone who had an attack of some sort or engine failure . Shortly thereafter I saw another plane coming in deliberately aiming at the second tower and realized it was an era ending plot to destroy American security and was I right? Of course, but what amazed me was the follow up details that revealed the pilots's quarters of these large potential death dealing airborne dangers to all including the paying passengers were WIDE OPEN TO ANYONE IN THE PLANE.

One hundred and twenty pound female flight attendants not trained in any particular method of karate or defensive strategies were basically the main defense against any nut, 200 or 300 pounds who might want to take the plane into a downward spin killing all aboard and people on the ground, for any reason, suicide, desire for notoriety,,sick and dying and insured for the flight.?

I realize this is a duplication of something written in an earlier portion of the book but I get sick and violently angry inside knowing that there were thousands of "security experts" who know about the lone muslim on a plane to Paris who almost destroyed the Eiffel tower as one man on a mission. By almost taking over the plane alone because the cock-pit was not locked ,amazing and disgusting uncaring Airline corporations.

What strikes me is the ardent avoidance of major airlines to avoid expending the necessary picayune amounts of money to secure the doors on all but the smallest planes against what we are now spending in time, equipment and personnel ,TRILLIONS over a short period AND YOUR GRANDCHILDREN WILL PAY IT.

Which brings me to my point,there is not a lawmaker alive who does not know in his soul that every civilized nation in the world has a national health plan that saves thousands of lives per years in each country but a vast percentage of our elected officials are resisting by every despicable means to destroy and avoid any improvement of the mess we now maintain . Much of the resistance is because of lobbyists who support these members of the best government money can buy to protect the status quo.

A fast look at Germany and Japan finds them decades ahead of the United States in overall healthplans, longer life ,lower birth deaths, less expenses by 30% on average and WE DESTROYED THESE COUNTRYS YEARS AGO TO A POINT THEY WERE DECIMATED.

How could we be so inertly stupid?

Remember when the health insurance companies and Harry and Sally spread TV poison against Hillrycare-? She was a woman so what could she know about healthcare?

And even now my friends believe all the negativity the Republican clone clowns can spout against any changes because they are born to believe in false leaders such as the despicables in Congress here and now, they helped elect them.

``The government will come between you and your doctor and there will be rationing and death panels."

The basics in America are the bottom line at the time, later we worry about future problems and costs. Clean it up later or " someone will, not me.""Deficits don't matter"

SHOTGUN Cheney,always so right for himself.

Woebegone Waretown   October 1 2009

The decades long government of only one party in our town has fallen apart .

Taxpayer citizens are paying a high price for this Toonerville self serving system.

Of course many of us can say "told ya so" since the 8 year reign of the national Republican party led us down the path of two 8 years wars unended and near bankruptcy as announced by the Republican Secretary of the Treasury in Sept. 2008 .

Common sense dictates there is a need for the checks and balances of a two party system.

Nationally this has been taken care of..

But here in Ocean Twp/Waretown we have the mayor under fire for profiting greatly on the Town Square, and an investigation is under way at his own request.

The former mayor has been indicted for accepting a bribe(later jailed)

The vice mayor has resigned,

The new highly paid administrator has been discharged behind closed doors by the council with no explanation or reason in less than a year' service although local newspaper articles give us some hints.

There are problems with the one remaining councilman having used public property to dock his boat at no charge for two years with the full knowledge of the township fathers.

So who is left?.

Waretown needs a Democratic council person or more. Perhaps an independent -ASAP

In the future we need to consider paying interested citizens more than a stipend to get more citizens involved in running for office so that those with hidden conflicts are not the only people running for office.

Why should over $120,000 go to one political appointee especially if he had to be discharged in less than a year?

Clearly the present system is far more costly than appears in the budget.

If the incumbent political party is perpetuated the voters can look forward to further expensive problems making a bad habit worse.

My neighbors should think hard on this or suffer the consequences .

Jack Doyle

WHILE I'M THINKING ABOUT IT only a one party town would allow such open graft GOP ,"GRAFT ON PARAADE"

CHAPTER 2

Failures with a destructive legacy –loudmouths speaking out with nothing to show for the party of NO.

Can anyone think of a proud accomplishment during the W years? Eight years of destruction of families,multiple interminable wars,the sinking economy and the country's reputation ,pride , future and standard of living went to hell.

In 2009 Republicans left standing from the bush administration speak out about their plans to destroy the recently elected President of the United States. Talk about"Obama's Waterloo"Now that's planning for all!

Could it be cause he's "other"?

It used to be the Two political parties came together after an election that pointed to a clear victor and coalesced around the leader of the nation and free world to better the 330 million citizens who live here who need government to help them rather than deceive them. Especially after the W "FIASCO''

But the republicans, bless them, who not only have nothing to offer now, they also show nothing for their 8 years of FAILURE when the Texas oil tar baby spoiled brat of politics led them down the path of Facism with torture ,wiretapping, unwinnable wars, massive debt for decades to come and hidden bankruptcy.(BUSH Wars were off-budget items)

Even as a far right commentator who has spoken for them for almost a decade,Bill O"Reilly, has praised President Obama they have publicly plotted the destruction of the President of the United States on the narrow grounds of Obama taking charge of things that have been left in the cesspool of ineptitude of 8 bush/cheney years of power and corporation government of and for the oil, war prof-iteers who supported it. In their eyes Obama cannot pos-sibly be doing things right and publicly they only give him a few months to correct the multiple errors of eight years.

Senator Dimwit from South Carolina and former Senate President Frist of the super wealthy Frists are cases in point. Look up Bill Frist and see where he has been and where he came from and why. His main purpose in poli-tics was to prevent national healthcare since his family was making billions as owners of the PROFITABLE hospital chain HCA.

Senator Dimwit from the least educated state in the Union has done nothing for the people who ignorantly elect him except act an outspoken member of the Peeparty . His opposition to national healthcare is vociferous in a state with no medical coverage for 30% of the population. Of course one must realize the demented one replaces the"cadaver" Senator from Tobacco Strom Thurmond who died in office at age of 104 serving fifty four consecutive years as Senator with impregnable financial backing from the smoking industry. You know, the cancer victim provider for treatment centers.

It should not be necessary to point out South Carolina is stuck in time, what era, it is hard to know.

A TALE OF TWO SHIFTY CITIES IN THE OCEAN COUNTY STICKIES

In Ocean County ,NJ there are two examples in close proximity to each other geographically and in time that point out the dangerous idiocy of having a one party system such as China, Russia, Cuba and other dictatorships have endured over decades.

The reason those countries have such a system is because violence is inflicted on those who oppose it. Instead of being ejected from a township meeting they can shoot you.

Here in Ocean County it exists because of citizen lethargy and the bad habit of believing one has been born with an R for republican on their butt. And that all R politicians are honest..

Most citizens of the United States now own a computer and are familiar with various search engines such as Google. You can look up what has happened in the Ocean Twp/Waretown government in the past six months and also look up what happened in Manchester Twp/Whiting about 18 years ago when the town was run by one party headed up by administrator Joseph Portash who died under indictment for fraud of nearly a million dollars with the municipality losing two million total in the end.

Among other acts of dishonesty several mayors wrote checks to themselves over a period of years for fraudulent reasons in amounts over thousands of dollars. Auditors seemed non existent overlooking this. Some things were caught later and punished ,some NOT.

It appears this is a good time for all voters in November to lose the R symbol on their voting forms and put someone in from the Democratic Party as watchdog over remaining incumbent dinosaurs .

The facts show how badly the town government needs this and soon. I refer to Waretown NJ the retired mayor of which has recently been sent to prison for accepting a $10,000. bribe in a "sting"operation. The subsequent mayor also a Republican resigned when it was revealed he had owner-ship of property under consideration for development by the township.This is typical of one party small towns in New Jersey and all over America, the land of privy opportunity.

Yet in Waretown senior citizen development newcom-ers from Northern NJ have flocked to the very party that screwed them in a move that puts a new slogan in practice,

" Even if you can beat them join them and enjoy the great Lobster Picnics" .

Small town graft and corruption is a well paying hobby for those so inclined in America. Unfortunately one of the antidotes to this has been the "Teaparty" with answers that include ignorance and extremism on a grand scale strangely mixed with honesty and genuine concern.

They really need help and so does this country.

JUST TO SHOW "HOW LONG HAS THIS BEEN GOING ON"

The United States Is In Deep Doodoo!

United States Congressional Record - March 17, 1993 - Vol. #33, page H-1303 - Speaker- Rep. James Traficant, Jr. (Ohio) addressing the House:

"Mr. Speaker, we are here now in chapter 11. Members of Congress are official trustees presiding over the greatest reorganization of any Bankrupt entity in world history, the U.S. Government. We are setting forth hopefully, a blueprint for our future. There are some who say it is a coroner's report that will lead to our demise."

NY TIMES

OP ED PAGE

620 8thAve.,NYC 10018   July15,2011

Dear Mr. Hoffman"

Regarding your OP ED of July 14th you say you are "Conservative" and you were partially responsible for George W.'s debacle of 2 losing wars of ten years and the Bankruptcy of the American economy? All in 8 years of fiasco ,lies and deceit. Conservatives need a dictionary. ,What was conservative about those years – so far right they were left they were! And WORSE YET you were with the NRC? Unbelievable, Any regrets considering?

Do you remember Republican Comptroller of the Treasury Walker leaving in disgust after many years of warning the administration and their corporate moneybaggers that the deficit was already equal to over $650,000. Per family in 2008? (worse now)

Smaller government you say, your coterie added tens of thousands of workers to the federal payrolls while sending tens of thousands of soldiers to the middle east to die while killing over 100,000 civilians and destroying a million homes in several countries. All to be rebuilt on our dollars. Conservative?

And for ten years no new jobs?And Republicans controlled both houses and the Whitehouse.

And Presently is it such news that the joker broker crafty money changer never elected Grover Nutwist is followed by the Koolaid sippers in your pee party? They belong to the Republicans who deserve them but not the American people ! What kind of cult followers are in your party? Sign a Pledge ? ,What are they drunks? I'm sure with your background you have no kinship with them ,golf does not mix with tea parties.

I worked briefly with an advisory committee for Governor Kean of New Jersey when he was first elected. After 8 years in office he doubled the number of State employees in 8 years. Conservative smaller government you say?

It will take100 years to even come close to balancing the US budget if ever , Stick around and see.

The last time America had no deficit was 1835, really no kidding. You could look it up.

JACK DOYLE

THIS LETTER NOT PRINTED BY THE NY TIMES

609 693 7441

A Look Back;

FIVE AND A HALF MONTHS INTO THE OBAMA ADMINISTRATION

And already people in polls were criticizing him for the GM and Chrysler "bailouts" (which started with ten billion in the Republican adminstration) and the national debt which was $700,000. per family before he was elected. Of course these are the same people who voted for georgie porgie bush TWICE who led us into two losing wars (one lost twice,THAT'S THREE WARS ,LOST)and borrowed trillions from Communist China but maintained an embargo on poverty stricken Cuba because of their human rights stands. The commies are still under Castro after fifty years.

- Is it possible W. bush .never heard of Tianamen square and forced abortions of China's infant girls?

- Apparently as just like Reagan who thought that dictator MARCOS of the Philippines amassed a multimillion dollar fortune by good investments while earning a salary of less than twenty grand per year. And Imelda's shoes were gifts! These guys were deliberately in a fog worse than London.!

- But talk about obtuse, most Americans now expect that corrections of the disasters inflicted in the past 8 years will be miraculous in the first year of a Democratic government and watch out, the mid term elections after a new party takes over always swing the other way against the new party in charge.

- And the talking heads of the R party who are not even members of the government(Nit Getrich, Rush Limpo, Handsome Hannetty, Richer than thou ex governor of Massachusetts, the savior of the Olympics with US government money, are now girding for a battle with lies and deceits beyond belief and the inbred red necks and corporate greedy-cats are right there with checkbooks hoping for more graft, oil and war profits and inside deals with a swing to the "right" in 2010.

- God forbid. But then what God would permit 280,000 innocent people to be swept away in a Japanese Tsunami or some 200,000 Iraqi civilians to be killed by Americans ("we don't keep a body count" Per a US General) and insurgents in the name of God, Freedom and Allah? Whose side are these multiple gods on?

- Lets face it, YOU CAN'T HANDLE THE TRUTH IF YOU WERE PART OF THE GROUP THAT VOTED REPUBLICAN TWICE FOR bushman WHOSE EVERY JOB WAS BOUGHT BY MONEY HE DID NOT EARN AND ACCOMPLISHED NOTHING IN THOSE POSITIONS, WHO ALSO WAS A DRAFT DODGER,A C STUDENT,CHEERLEADER AND DRUNK DRIVER UNTIL HE WAS THIRTY.(as Casey Stengel said "you could look it up")

- But Americans are Suckers so don't put it past the R party to pick up some power in at least governor's posts in some states such as New Jersey where I reside.

- The blame for loss of jobs in NJ is being put on the incumbent Dem governor in ads run by the challenger although the rate of unemployment is 20 percent below the national average and of course is due to a world-wide Republican recession/depression that will stick around for many years because the party of NO wants to keep things heading downhill, better for them in the next election.

2 Dirty Rotten Scoundrels The NRC and Carl Rove

This organized bunch of money power hungry pirates of America has done many con jobs on the people of America and the Democratic party has let them do it because in my opinion they feel that there is a right of"FREE SPEECH" to do so but a hesitation to do the same in retribution or reaction on their part. This attitude has to change

The NRC mails out talking points(or stalking points) on a regular basis on subjects that they feel may make them look bad or aggressively on subjects that they wish to pursue ad infinitum .

Republican "talking heads" use every opportunity to talk over or voice over discussions by those they oppose at every chance even after they have had their say and the other party is to speak uninterrupted during radio or TV interviews with 2 sides supposedly represented fairly.

These tactics are picked and packed by smart craft men like Carl Rove, an expert in propaganda, manipulation , cunning half truths and outright lies.

GREED RULES, NOT THE GOLDEN RULE !

A man I knew and was related to by marriage some years ago worked as construction contractor for a worldwide major Hotel-Motel chain and would take part in sit down meetings with the owner concerning plans for new buildings all over America. He was on a first name basis with Bill and had many meetings and dinners with him over a period of 20 years as a member of the top executive echelon.

I was reliably informed the rule laid down by this owner THROUGHOUT was when traveling people who worked for his firm were to stay in the Sheraton motels because their own rates were too high.

This is similar to Mayor Bloomburg and the NYC chamber of commerce being against the paying of a ten dollar per hour living wage to workers in the city because it would be harmful to Manhattan business. Religious institutions are trying to get this living wage practice established in New York City universally and are meeting with political and business leaders as this is wrtten.

The question arises if all firms were to avoid paying a living wage what consuming population would continue the revenue stream necessary to keep any business functioning and profitable? And so we see the ethos of the gap between the one percent and the 99% of have nots and it does not emanate from the latter.

Greed continues to flourish in the hearts and minds of billionaires.

Some very wealthy citizens who have the general well being of the nation in mind such as Bill Gates of Microsoft,Warren Buffett of his own conglomerate industries are in favor of paying higher taxes as they know in their hearts and minds that the current tax system is heading over a cliff without massive design change and the wealthy and corporations are required to pay a fairer larger share of profits to put the world economy on a sound footing over the next 50 years. Polls show almost 80% of those with incomes over one million favor this idea.

It is evident without more money in the pockets of the 90 percent of wage earners who have lost a crucial 10 to 20% of income in the past decade there will be less youth heading to college and specialty schools to maintain the knowledge bank of industry and commerce supplying innovation,design and executive capacity for American businesses. The ignorance of Rick Sanitarium be damned!

Further,the health and welfare of American employees, their retirement funding must be accommodated in the income from a normal work week. Workers cannot be expected to work part time after a 35 or 40 hour week in their prime occupation .Americans should not be forced for profit of the one percent to come down to the level of third world or developing countries.To prevent this tariffs and quotas are in order as they existed in Reagan's time controlling Japanese and German auto imports.

In March of 2012 a shockingly bipartisan (Yes 379 No 39) Congress passed a law enabled countervailing duties on Chinese and Vietnamese products that are subsidized by those countries. Products made in the USA will now be equal in pricing.Hopefully this is the start of realization that American manufacturers need help against manipulated foreign products. MANUFACTURING USED TO REPRESENT OVER THIRTY PERCENT OF GNP,IN 2012 IT IS TWELVE!

It is disgusting to note that the US minimum wage has been adjusted only infrequently in the past fifty years. Apparantly adjustment according to the cost of living never occurred to our LESS THAN magnanimous Congress . Here's the recent history of our slave like pay rates, it is fortunate some of our states exceed federal requirements which have not been adjusted since July 2009. Note the ten year gap from 1997 to 2007.

09/01/1997	$5.15
07/24/2007	$5.85
07/24/2008	$6.55
07/24/2009	$7.25

Even more miserly is the rate for workers under age of 20 who are paid $4.25 per hour for the first 120 days .Currently regular workers age 20 and over are paid $7.25 per hour. Try renting a house anywhere in America for a family of four with that. No damn wonder poverty has increased in the past decade and people need food stamps.

If higher wages cause modest inflation that would be good for the nation, check the opinion of economists. The current mode is bad bad bad for America and has been for DECADES.

PLEDGE OF ALLEGIANCE TO WHAT FLAG ?
GROVER NUTCASE

As interested and involved in politics as I have been for 60 years Dear Grover, the savior of conservatism according to himself has pretty much escaped my attention until now when suddenly Republican candidates and elected officials have become a cult, worshipping at his doctrines. This reflects on the quality of life in a Democracy because there never has been an elected office this character has achieved.

In viewing this self centered pompous nutcase for the first time he really is dislikeable putting it mildly.And this is without knowing he was born rich and feathered his own nest with Rich peoples's money.

He drips in repulsive associations such as convicted Lobbyist Jack Abramoff,Get out the vote groups in college for Nixon,(Did they drink and chase checks or chicks ?) groups against healthcare reform extending back to Clinton's era,of course including Obama's Healthcare law, the Oliver North illegal Contras ,the Christian Coalition (they really claim to be Christians),the National Rifle Association ,William Christol (Doesn't he do a nice Oscar Emcee) ,Ralph Reed.,the more than right but incorrect Americans For Tax Reform, Newt Getrich, Carl Rove, Go Proud ,the Nixon Center(remember Tricky Dicky escaping on a helicopter prior to near impeachment) enough already- to gag me. There's more.

THE FARMERS OF THE CONSTITUTION

They owned people of darker skin than residents of America at that time. These darker skinned human beings were totally bound to the farmers who were among the wealthier and better educated whites of the time , interested in the freedoms they sought mostly because they felt such a form of government would benefit them personally and as a group

These wealthy property owning farmers historically became known as the " Framers of the constitution ".This group had come to the conclusion they would be better off without the distant direction of royalty in England and they broadcast cries of "tyranny" as best they could considering there were no means of communication nationally or internationally without long delays .

As we all know newspapers, the few that there were and letters took a long time to disseminate throughout the colonies and of course posting letters back to England took portions of a year by sailing ship.

The people who started this uprising were know as revolutionaries and they were outnumbered by the people who were loyalists to England and the Monarchy of the British throne.

This writer ate many meals and hoisted a number of libations at the King George Inn in the Watchung Mountains of NJ, gathering place for Loyalists and a Stage coach stop in the mid to late1700's.

To Continue, Let's not rock the boat they said to themselves but only for so long.

There were no Gallup polls then but perhaps "gallop -polls" such as queries to travelers on horseback "What's happening in your neck of the woods"spread the news of this unheard of usurping of English rule.

Some structures in America still stand where meetings were held by both Revolutionaries and Tories (loyalists) especially on the Eastern seaboard in States like Mass, NJ ,NY ,PA .Philadelphia is a prime city full of buildings vital to the birth of American freedom and the Constitution was written, signed and printed there under the auspices and direction of Benjamin Franklin, the nation's first printer and a genius slaveholder.

Small wars much like gang wars were fought between both sides before the larger scale revolt with organized broad efforts took place.

If these skirmishes were to take place today constables and "an organized militia" would be called upon to quell the side fighting against the crown, (kind of like the Crips and the Bloods) and there were in many areas more militia than anti British residents.

But the economic benefits of throwing off taxes paid to England with the idea of "freedom" from a form of government that formed by circumstance of birth rather than

reasoned order began to form a concensus driven stronger effort than England was able to rebuff from so far away .

After the end of the war the first American president George Washington declared a precedent setting disdain for personal succession to leadership of the new nation setting up the system of elections after the end of his agreed eight year term.his desire was to return to farming in Virginia. Picture that today !

Mayor Bloomberg of NYC has since disagreed with this theory of leadership feeling there is more reason to continue in office past 8 years than to seek higher office or return his efforts to commerce .

CHAPTER 3

Justin case you missed it !

 REAGAN MYTH . . . The Progressive Review

prorev.com/reagan.htm

Reagan conducted one of the most absurd **invasions** of **American** history, targeting the tiny Island, GRANADA.which covered up for Reagan's previous decision to send troops to **Lebanon that cost** 241 Marine lives AND RESULTED IN A ONE MONTH LATER EVACUATION which he said resulted in a more "defensible position" It truly was a defeat but Granada was a PR move that changed the headlines.(ALSO COST MORE DEAD SOLDIERS)

The Reagan Years

	1977–80	1981–83	CHANGE
Real GNP	+3.2%	+1.3%	−59%
Industrial Production	+3.0%	+0.1%	−97%
Rate of Capacity Utilization	83.4%	75.9%	− 9%
Plant & Equipment Expenditures	+14.6%	.8%	−95%
Housing Starts	1.76mil	1.28mil	−27%
Domestic Auto Sales	8.48mil	6.25mil	−26%
Business failures	8461	24491	+189%
Civilian unemployment	6.5%	9.0%	+ 38%
Number of persons unemployed	6.74mil	9.89mil	+ 47%
Real disposable income	+1.9%	+1.3%	− 32%
Prime Rate	10.96%	14.84%	+35%
Federal Budget deficit	$48.5bil	$153.0bil	+215%
Farm Income	+1.75%	−5.7%	−326%

(Source: Congressional Record, 3/26/84. Each figure is an overall or annual average in order to offset any difference which would arise due to the variance in the number of years of each administration.

historical. THE COST OF OUR UNUSED AND USELESS ATOMIC WEAPONS AS OF 1996 ADD 25% FOR 2012

AND WE USED TWO OF THEM OVER 70YEARS AGO. TRANSLATED THISISCLOSE TO SEVEN TRILLION 300 BILLION DOLLARS AND MORE SINCE A CONSTANT 1996 DOLLAR HAS DEPRECIATED

Total: $5,821.0 billion

in billions of constant 1996 dollars

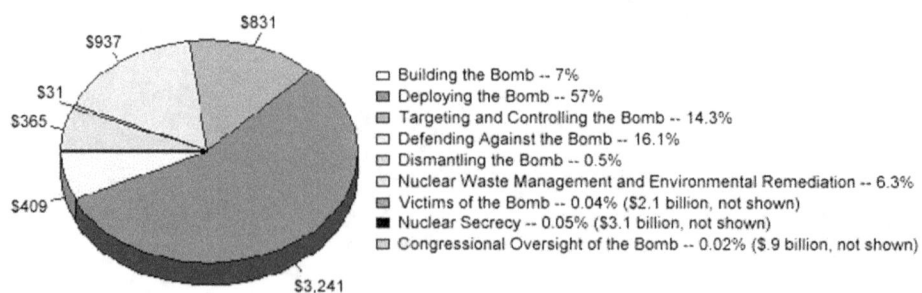

- Building the Bomb -- 7%
- Deploying the Bomb -- 57%
- Targeting and Controlling the Bomb -- 14.3%
- Defending Against the Bomb -- 16.1%
- Dismantling the Bomb -- 0.5%
- Nuclear Waste Management and Environmental Remediation -- 6.3%
- Victims of the Bomb -- 0.04% ($2.1 billion, not shown)
- Nuclear Secrecy -- 0.05% ($3.1 billion, not shown)
- Congressional Oversight of the Bomb -- 0.02% ($.9 billion, not shown)

*Includes average projected future-year costs for nuclear weapons disman-
tlement and fissile materials disposition and environmental remediation and
waste management. Total actual and estimated expenditures through 1996
were $5,481.1 billion.

Source: *Atomic Audit: The Costs and Consequences of U.S. Nuclear Weapons
Since 1940* (Brookings Institution Press, 1998)

Copyright © 1998 The Brookings Institution

REPUBLICANS SHOW AND TELL THE WORLD WHAT THEY ARE !

Almost a year ago at the outset of the pointless ignorant
and nearly endless argument about HEALTHCARE REFORM
one of the leading Republican Senators, Senator Dimint of
South Carolina stated " This will be his Waterloo" referring to
President Obama and his efforts to pass reform in any sensible fashion

This has been because every effort was made by the entire
Republican party to confuse,complicate and destroy any
effort in regard to improving healthcare delivery to the US
public and the idea became a will of the wisp CONSTANTLY
MORPHING in the eyes of the general public because of
fabrications, exaggerations and outright lies about the plan
from the start by all Republican party members.

Sen. Dimint's statement was not denied or contradicted
by any Republican member of party or Congress, in other
words it was outright war by any means on any plan to
improve American healthcare in any form as long as it was
connected to Obama and his administration and party.

There were no suggestions to work together or sit down and
plan.

This demonstrates that all Republicans prefer some 15,000 to 20,000 people dying for lack of care EVERY YEAR!, 500,000 Americans declaring bankruptcy due to inability to pay for medical bills every year and in addition one million people losing their homes to foreclosure because of inability to pay medical bills.

This party prefers the status quo of insurance companies to deny coverage to people who are sick and unemployed and to put a limit on the insurance coverage paid for any sickness no matter how progressive or debilitating the illness.

It is a FACT also in New Jersey that the leading flagholder The Corpulent Christie ,governor of the Republican party would prefer less teachers, closed schools, crowded class-rooms, extra sessions AND HIGHER LOCAL TAXES so he can cut taxes for wage earners of $400,000 per year, the top wealthiest of the state.

One billion dollars for the richest group who supported him in the election. Zip for all others.

This shows where he puts his love and priorities. That's the Republican party.

What a loverly bunch of coconuts.

THE AUDACITY OF ASSES

In September of 2009 Fox News had the brass gonads to run TV ads of a Nationally inspired "Tea Party" they claimed were not given any coverage by other news networks. The American viewing public was sickened by constant scenes of idiotically dressed marchers in a mob scene in Washington, DC carrying signs accusing President Obama of being a Communist, Socialist, Racist or any combination of same.

Many of the attendees there were anywhere from 7 years of age to 12 or 15 or retirees .accompanied by speeches from Republican elected officials including Sen. Demented from South Carolina.

Needless to say the other networks responded further casting the falsehoods across the TV screens and Internet networks of the land showing how they indeed did broadcast these "people" exercising their "rights" not only to speak but be wrong while sponsored by industries and politicians that had their own agendas carried by the ignorant assemblages.

Much of the panoply reminded the writer of the beer hall putsch of Munich in the 1930's as it has been described many times in history..

And we are stuck with this pack of idiots for the future until they are found out. More on them later.

NIXON FAMOUSLY STATED "I WILL GO TO CHINA"(1971)

Nixon " I am not a crook"(1973)

Nixon did his historic China trip for sensible and infinitely wise reasons and the statement about not being a crook was a bald faced lie. The history of the world was changed by bringing the Chinese to the economic bargaining table.

If the Watergate burglary had not taken place the course of the Nixon presidency would have proceeded smoothly and the course of his administration and the historical judgment of his rule would have been far kinder . Gerald Ford would have been nominated and elected president without the stain of the ex post facto pardon and probably he would have been fairly elected and muddled through as did Nixon.

A Republican friend of mine criticized Nixon for setting up China for more diplomatic and business ties with us. I argued that the best way to treat a powerful adversary was to make yourself important enough so they would try to prevent any harm coming to you because of self interest.

As everyone knows at this juncture Nixon was under threat of impeachment and resigned,naming Ford as president and was in turn" pardoned" for any possible crimes he" may" have committed. He wrote a book in retirement in Saddle River ,NJ.

If China had any intent of military action against the United States it would do them more harm than good if we were to become economically important to them, forcing us to become military adversaries would preclude our rich market ever being available to their cheaper but well made goods A war would have devastated both sides and the world.

Sadly over the years this hybrid capitalistic oriented Communist dictatorship has become a major source of mercantile products and also has provided the recent bush administration with funds to enable the suicidal tax cuts for the wealthy and the deficit funding for 2 wars without purpose or end. This has been a building block of our dungeon of debt.

People who used to make these goods stateside have been relegated to lower paying jobs or have become a large population of underemployed and/or welfare assisted unhappy citizens of the United States .Retraining has been a mostly futile effort for people in the

South, middle West and urban parts of America .Estimates are Ten Million such folks.

It can safely be said China's pathological fear of anything resembling democracy detracts fatally from their efforts and their ambivalent form of government prevents them from providing the freedom that many of their young people are seeking as they provide the intelligence and labor necessary to build this nation of one and half billion people into the major power they seek.

Recently it has been noted by our fiscal people that China has lessened the manipulation of their currency which is what we have been seeking for years, this may well be self preservation movement on their part to prevent an Obama administration and Congress from writing "protectionist " laws that ad tariffs to Chinese goods.

What would the effect of higher prices by 2 to 3% on all Chinese goods be to our current "recession(depression)" Let's see where we can go and how to achieve it.

Tariffs must be applied now and sensibly on selected products or our manufacturers are going down lower than the 13% of GNP retained now.

THE PEE PARTY ORIGINS

The intellectual (?)Basis for theory and substance)More on this later.

Perhaps never in the history of American Politics has this nation seen such a collection of misfits duly nominated and elected to run for important offices in the primaries of one of the two major parties as this year of 2010.

The first major advertisement of our erstwhile Republican prospective Senator from the little State of Delaware denies she is a witch. Sadly for her she brought it up in a previous TV interview with Bill Maher mentioning she had dabbled in witchcraft while in college,- she had claimed a degree from as long ago as 1995 but just qualified for same in the past three months .More levity about her is available but why beat a dead mouse.(oh yeah, she decries masturbation and has never married)

Disgustingly and shockingly polls show she is within 16 points of her competitor which makes one wonder about the intellectual level in the population of Delaware. Being a small State is really no excuse and her being a cute looking forty year old on Television does not qualify a "girl"who has never had a real paying job as candidate for a Senate position.

Then we proceed to another "Momma Grizzly" (so named by Sarah Palin) Sharon Angle of Nevada who has publicly called for people to "take up arms" if she is not elected to the office of Senator. Her handicap besides being incredibly naïve (for instance should NV folks shoot at their own kids in the Army in the case of her armed insurrection) is she would supplant the Speaker of the House if elected and have no seniority or clout to benefit her state for years to come. She has declared Social Security should be privatized or replaced (?),The tax code should be replaced with a flat tax ,the US should get out of the United Nations and the Department of Education disbanded among other things requiring a century of changes. Her counterclaim to her lack of seniority is she is respected by Sen. Jim Dimwit, the arch conservative of South Carolina which could get her some boiled peanuts and an immediate audience with Jim when needed.This is her "angle".

Then there is Rand Paul of Kentucky (another Pee party darling) the eye doctor myopic son of Ron Paul.

Look up this clown's budget plan introduced in the Senate which includes cutting Social Security by 40% and ending Medicare within two years and reducing income taxes to 17%. And this nightmare scheme drew 12 yes votes in the Senate of the United States of America ! Shows all of the nutcases are not in the Sanitarium.

WHITEHOUSE CONSIDERS FOX NEWS THE ENEMA

Yes, that could be a Freudian slip on my part but it seems that is a true to life definition of the way that so called news organization is defined by the Obama people and rightfully so. It is hard to believe that one of the top Irritants at faux FoxNews actually wrote a glowing three page article extolling the virtues of Barak Obama for Parade Magazine, the Sunday supplement that has a massive circulation during the third quarter of 2009.

The essence of the piece was and I quote,"If not Obama then who?"

Now in January of 2012 we shall see who Bill O'Reilly favors in the office, the Faux news is prepping with new strikes against the enemy Democrat that ended the Bush wars and soon tax cuts for the wealthy all without tapping phone lines.

CHAPTER 4

PERTINENT COMMENTS

CREDIT Garry Dorrien, Columbia University

The teaparty (Peeparty) exploded into being by claiming that Obama's mildly Keynesian stimulus of $787 billion was anti-American and Socialist. We had lost nearly 3 million jobs the previous year, we lost 741,000 in the month that Obama was inaugurated, and the economy was free-falling into a Depression. Even Republican economists contended that the U.S. desperately needed a Keynesian infusion to stop the economy from spiraling into an abyss. But somehow it was horribly wrong to save the nation from reliving 1933. On the basis of this absurd position every House Republican voted against Obama's stimulus and the Tea Party subsequently won a tremendous political windfall -- which has made the Republican Party more extreme than ever.

The Tea Party is overwhelmingly white, middle-class, and either middle-aged or elderly. It thrives on a deeply felt dichotomy between the deserving and the undeserving. At the grassroots level, much of the Tea Party is not hostile to Social Security or Medicare, unlike the professional ideologues that are exploiting it. Tea Party Republicans are quite certain that they deserve their own Social Security and

Medicare. But they are outraged that undeserving people get taxpayer-funded benefits from the government. In the Tea Party version of the American dream, there is no such thing as the common good. There is only the sum of individual goods, which many people do not deserve.

The Right-wing anti-Obama literature charges incessantly that white liberals coddled an undeserving Obama into and through Harvard Law School, financed his political career, and fawned over him all the way to the White House, where he betrays America's national interests and slathers the undeserving with Obamacare and food stamps. The Tea Party, a new phenomenon, capitalizes on resentments and a mean-spirited ideology that are far from new in U.S. American life

Author DOYLE COMMENT; - Are the Tea Party cultists suffering from dementia? Or is there something narcotic in their tea? It is a fact most of them think the US should default on our credit obligations. Worse yet one of their Elected leaders ,Michelle Backward feels that the Treasurer of the United States can gather all of the funds on hand at one time and devote it to paying off part of the national deficit in one swift movement., avoiding facts of other debts due. This is the type of thinking at the forefront of one of their leading illusionary intellects.And she ran for President and has been elected to Congress three terms. EEEEEGAWDS!

But the idea that we owe obligations to each other to serve the common good is equally long-standing in American history and politics. A federal budget is a moral document. If we scaled back America's global military empire and reinstated a morally decent tax system and budget, we could eliminate the entire federal debt by 2021 without cutting Social Security, Medicare, Medicaid, education, or research.

A decent system would have additional brackets for the highest incomes, as the U.S. once did. It would have a bracket for $1 million earners and a bracket for $10 million dollar earners and a bracket for $100 million earners and so on. It would lift the cap on the regressive Social Security tax, taxing salaries above $110,000 per year. It would tax capital gains as ordinary income. It would cap the benefit on itemized deductions at 28 percent. It would tax U.S. foreign income as it is earned. It would eliminate the subsidies for oil, gas, and coal companies. It would place a tax on credit default swaps and futures and charge a leverage tax on the megabanks.

These are not radical proposals. If we adopted all of them, we would still be well below European levels of taxation. All of them together merely, mildly restore the principle that people should pay taxes on the basis of their ability to do so – a principle that polls very well even in red states.

Gary Dorrien is Reinhold Niebuhr Professor of Social Ethics at Union Theological Seminary and Professor of Religion at Columbia University. His 16 books include "Kantian Reason and Hegelian Spirit" (Wiley-Blackwell, 2012) and the recently published "The Obama Question: A Progressive Perspective" (Rowman & Littlefield).

IF AL GORE BECAME PRESIDENT

Does anyone with half a brain think that Al Gore as a president would have invaded the wrong country, Iraq, sent many more troops there and ignored the need for a peacekeeping force in Afghanistan after our initial effort in putting the Taliban down.?

Then you are a sick puppy Republican and go to the ass end of the class.

Any more weird thinking?

Then of course we would not have had tax cuts for the richest five percent of the earning and investing public and would have had far less casualties in our armed forces, no lobbyists in charge of departments they were supposed to oversee and improve,there would be no 800 million dollar embassy in Iraq and a need for ten thousand people paid by America to defend and staff it for decades to come.

Further there would be no 200,000 dead Iraq civilians, 250,000 widowed Iraq women living in tents in squalor, the oil producing countries would not have increased our cost of oil by 250% and inflation here would have been far lower than encountered in the bush 8 years.

American armed forces casualties could have been held to a minimum and our deficit would have been less than half of what occurred.

Is all of this Because obedient party serving Justices appointed by bush's Father were obligated to decide the Republican way?What a fatal blow to the American people ! appointed by Daddy Bush was destined to select between W.Bush and Al Gore? YES , How stupid could we be?

SEE HOW IMPORTANT YOUR VOTE CAN BE?

Reagan all but appointed George Bush president since he was his VP and the establishment supported him even though he lied in his teeth about being "out of the loop" in the mess created by the arms to Iran supported in secret by his own party illegally in order to release hostages of Iran. Reagan was Pinnochio as well.

National Security Archive Electronic Briefing Book No. 365 (from the Internet)

A detailed report report on Bush's involvement does, however, shed considerable light on his role in both the Iran and Contra sides of the scandal. The memorandum on criminal liability noted that Bush had a long involvement in the Contra war, chairing the secret "Special Situation Group" in 1983 which "recommended specific covert operations" including "the mining of Nicaragua's rivers and harbors." (Researcher) Mixter also cited no less than a dozen meetings that Bush attended between 1984 and 1986 in which illicit aid to the Contras was discussed.

Bush when he was president pardoned everyone except the kitchen help for their Contra actions in case they were guilty similar to President Ford's pardon of Nixon "in case".

That seems a Republican forte similar to unaffordable tax cuts to win an election.

This is the history of the GOP!

DUMBOCRACY NOT AS ENVISIONED

Another glaring lack in the Democratic system is the lack of incentive for citizens to cast votes diluting the good and promoting the bad in governance.

More than a dozen states have passed laws in Republican legislatures through various subterfuges like requiring a photographic " votercard" or a birth certificate by those casting a vote.These new "voter fraud" laws seek to disenfranchise the poor and elderly,college students and the young who have difficulty in accessing such documents.

The pretext of voter fraud is fraud itself as there is no evidence of more than a few illegally cast votes in any elections in all covered voting districts over the past decade. This concerted effort is directed by Carl Rove to prevent

Democratic votes now and in the future. The Federal election commission now is seeking to overturn these transparent efforts to control elections.

Some nations have a penalty for not voting and get a participation rate in the 90

percentile range, In a less demanding America we should give an incentive of tax credits for voting in National and state elections increasing them after for instance 5 continuous votes, then ten, etc. Such a plan would encourage more interest in candidates' views and keep voters up on the promises made and kept in selected election campaigns as time goes on.

Participative Democracy is badly needed here as witness where the majority of citizens until late 2008 thought that Saddam Hussein had responsibility for the Twin Towers destruction, also that we had found weapons of mass destruction in Iraq. FOX ?

Such ignorance is unconscionable except for the fact that the Republican administration propaganda machine deliberately kept these myths alive for as long a they could including outright lying whenever possible.

While I'm at it with reference to faults in American democracy the Jury system is another problem that needs attention that no one in authority is willing to give it.

Adversary proceedings with winner take all thrust (guilty or not guilty) encourage prosecutors to withhold evidence, coach witnesses to lie and simply adopt a winner take all attitude and the same holds true for poorly paid defense councils who are many times appointed by law to the " indigent."

Cuts in budgets on all levels threaten capable legal reps for those who cannot afford one.

Juries do not have the technical knowledge they need to settle and adjudicate complicated scientific and medical cases and must rely on evidence without referring to further study or testimony of unbiased scientists,doctors ,specialists etc. who have no self interested point to make.They are in all cases paid by one side or the other and dueling experts confuse jurors.

Juries cannot question witnesses or dueling attorneys.

The Menendez Brothers and O.J. Simpson trials in California were a perfect example of the twisting of justice because juries were subpar in performance intellectually.

Many Countries have trial by a jury of pro jurists, judges who know the law and can ask questions at appropriate times which jurors can not .All courtroom actors are seeking justice and the truth and represent the public interest though the defense will take the side that makes the defendant look innocent as much as possible.

Another poorly thought out facet of our justice system is the election of judges based on advertising and campaigns by the candidates who in many county (parish) or townships are not required to have any legal education whatsoever .They can be tailors, mechanics or farmers and as long as they say the pleasing(politic) thing in their campaigns and get enough votes-----------

"HERE COME THE JUDGE."

A recent case that was a miscarriage of justice had to be brought to the Supreme Court to make it right. Even there the case was close, the decision was split 5 to 4 involving a case in the West Virginia supreme court Chief Justice Brennan presiding. Brennan after having benefited from THREE MILLION DOLLARS spent on advertising advocating his reelection by the defendant Massey Coal.

Brennan did not recuse himself from a decision that threw out a FIFTY MILLION DOLLAR award to be paid by Massey to the plaintiff coal companies who were harmed by fraud by the big spending Massey defendant.

Sadly most Americans are unaware that KING COAL ,ASTHMA INDUCER IS SEEKING TO RULE THE LAND led by the ever prominent greedy Koch Brothers, multibillion dollar corporation.

The sophistry of the claim that the first amendment supporting free speech as it has newly been interpreted by the corporately controlled United States Supreme Court enables advertising for candidates for any office and in this case a judge as long as that service is not paid by the candidate. This masquerade makes free speech an expansive WEALTH DRIVEN right of the wealthiest as opposed to a small group of 2 or 200 people who can only afford a dollar per person while another can spend millions through "focus groups" or facades of many kinds

They "focus" all right. Spelled with --ck .

UNEMPLOYMENT CURRENT WORRY-COMPARE THE REAGAN DEPRESSION

Under Obama after less than 7 month in office assorted R critics of the administration point to a rate of joblessness that is still lower than that during the 1981-1983 period and criticize the Democrat for what is obviously a result of the past 8 years of R ineptitude

Fighting two wars 7000 miles away from home with little help from our "friends" and keeping the cost of those two wars "off budget'' as if they were bad dreams never to be accounted for on the ledger sheet.

Keeping the vast majority of the labor force at no increase in pay for 8 years of course added greatly to the problem.

BUT the Reagan years were far worse and you can look it up. Let this be your assignment in econ history research.(ten percent for several years)

The prime point here is that it was an R Sec of Treasury appointed by the bumbling bush, who called Congressional and financial officials into one room and announced that credit had dried up in America and about a TRILLION DOLLARS WAS NEEDED TO BAIL OUT OUR PROBLEMS AND NOW.!(It started out at 700 billion and grew like a Chia pet)

History will show Sec. Of Treasury Paulson was one of five people who helped set up the horrific swaps and derivative system that cause the mess we are now in. It is also important to know that when he took the appointment by bush he saved many millions in taxes since he was forced to divest large portions of his fortune to accept a government post , The tax code permits him to leave private employment without tax penalty..

Fifty million or so tax free at a time when he perhaps knew the excreta was about to hit the fan? Good lottery ticket I would say.

So mid 2009 we are still in the R soup waiting for Obama's plan to rescue us .It will probably take until mid century before we see a leveling out of the entire economy and housing will start to make a weak but important upward movement .Because Home sales and permits are the most important building block in our econ along with car and truck sales more years of misery will be in store.

Now to the main thrust of this portion of our story, the weakened but still financially strong Republicans will pull out all stops and disregard truth in their advertising and public pronouncements casting aspersions against Obama and his team making the Democrats responsible for all that goes wrong with the world and original sin.

The twist in this is the people who are working with the new president were in the Repugnican party cadre in the past and now are responsible for pulling us out of the disaster they helped create.This would be Paul the cigar Volcker, Sec. Of Treasury Geithner , Exuberance Greenspan and others.

As Time goes by the cast of characters will change and results of the tractor pull will change for the better as the drain of two wars is hopefully lessened.

Even after agreeing to reduce Pentagon spending by a trillion dollars last fall the Republicans at this writing are trying to add HALF A TRILLION DOLLARS back into the deficit for their supporters in the military industrialist complex!

At that point our defenses pending at 650Billion does not amount to much more than 650% higher than China's 110 Billion.

Meantime the Guns On Parade party will still decry wasteful spending and the deficit showing their clever use of fun house mirrors much like candidate Romney.

An update as of Feb.2012 - jobs data is finally showing an uptrend toward 8% and lower... The Chamber of Commerce dictate not to hire unless you have to from the mandate mouth Senator Turtle McConnell("to make Obama a one term president") cannot be held firm and Republican plans to obstruct everything beneficial to Americans to make Democrats look bad is reflecting back on the perpetrators according to polls showing Congress with a less than ten percent approval rating.!

Paul Krugman in the NY Times recently pointed out;

", what about jobs? I have to admit that I started laughing when I saw The Wall Street Journal offering North Dakota as a role model. Yes, the oil boom there has pushed unemployment down to 3.2 percent, but that's only possible because the whole state has fewer residents than metropolitan Albany — so few residents that adding a few thousand jobs in the state's extractive sector is a really big deal. The comparable-sized fracking boom in Pennsylvania has had hardly any effect on the state's overall employment picture, because, in the end, not that many jobs are involved.

And this tells us that giving the oil companies carte blanche isn't a serious jobs program. Put it this way: Employment in oil and gas extraction has risen more than 50 percent since the middle of the last decade, but that amounts to only 70,000 jobs, around one-twentieth of 1 percent of total U.S. employment. So the idea that drill, baby, drill can cure our jobs deficit is basically a joke.

Why, then, are Republicans pretending otherwise? Part of the answer is that the party is rewarding its benefactors: the oil and gas industry doesn't create many jobs, but it does spend a lot of money on lobbying and campaign contributions. The rest of the answer is simply the fact that conservatives have no other job-creation ideas to offer.

And intellectual bankruptcy, I'm sorry to say, is a problem that no amount of drilling and fracking can solve."

ECONOMICS AS WE KNOW THE SUBJECT-THE BLIND CAN VOTE.

To think that the American public can form an intelligent opinion on the subject matters that relate to the Obama administration moves since Democrats took office is to believe in Santa and the tooth fairy. But then everyone has an opinion-is it justified?

After all the government has spent billions in advisors and analysts over the past half century and look where we are in the location of the fiscal dumpster, the United States is at the bottom with previous enemies Japan and Germany as just a few examples in fairly good shape. Didn't we destroy them, including two A bombs on Japan?

Many, not all Nations that have not been police to the world are far ahead of us in balancing their budgets and enabling their populations to lead happy and productive lives.

The sad truth is on a happiness scale we are at the bottom (sorry folks but it's true).

For the facts see other parts of this book. But then, if you read other than the headlines ,sports and the comics you already know the facts..

A Nobel prize winning economist has written what the Democratic administration has done in "BAILING OUT" has prevented a deepening of the recession/depression but perfect solutions to the causes of this mess have not occurred because of deliberate obstructionism.. The problem is the stim was not large enough because of Republicans who are still in the1930's.

We should point out the same brilliant writer was around when banks and AIG,etc. and Congress were creating this miscarriage but what good could he as one man do?

Progress takes time. Disaster can happen almost overnight .Witness the ``W" Bush ."appointment" by his Fathers friend on the Supreme Court , his administration and the power grabbers placed in key positions during the horrendous 8 years in office and their decisions about many subjects like Iraq,Banking,Commerce and Taxes.

The Bush cut in taxes for the wealthy was supposed to bring forth more jobs than ever before but in 8 years the most we saw was 2 ½ million while millions more went overseas to China and other Asian countries.

In comparison,.

The 8 years of the Clinton Presidency showed over 22 million jobs created and this was after a small increase in taxes at he start of the 8 years which resulted in balanced budgets for four of the years and nearly balanced budgets in the first half of the administration.

Enourmous deficits were a result of the Bush tax reduction on oil and gas,firms,lower levies on higher incomes, capital gains and inheritances during the prosecution of two 8 year wars put our economic structure in the toilet. Especially since the majority of lower and middle class wage earners lost a large percentage of their income during that period therefore consumers of goods and services in the US could not afford to keep the economy going - well demonstrated by what followed.

Bush's Treasury Sec..Paulson finally came clean (FORCED BY REALITY) and announced the problem in his Sept. 2008 meeting with all of the money people in government and banking ,the world watching,. Credit had come to a grinding halt for the nation's borrowers ,individuals and corporate.

This was as close to an announcement of bankruptcy of a world power as had been heard since the Soviet Union collapse.. The situation was a perfect storm for the nation as a whole, we were sinking and a new Commander was not yet at the helm.

Ultimately the Obama reaction certainly was better then what we saw in the previous eight years and will be improved upon though gradually and with the help of many more intelligent members of his line and staff who do not have an agenda designed to put most of the nation's wealth in the hands of the top 1%.- Democratic plans were not secretly designed to help the stocks in the coffers of any group of Wall Street Funds as had been the case.

At the outset in 2008 Obama was placed in the most difficult situation with the weakest economic options at his command as any US president in history and the structure of the nation's economy was at the worst ever. Bush's mistakes in foreign policy and war mismanagement, cutting taxes during their prosecution were crippling to all who followed and yet someone had to take over. Thank heavens and the voters it was not part of the dynasty establishment.

FREEDOM FROM INTELLIGENT DECISIONS

In 2007 the decision was made by the Bush administration to convert the light bulb industry to an energy saving form that will conserve at least 25% of the energy used in previous models. That decision to be in effect in 2010 made by a Republican administration is now being contradicted by a diminished thinking "freedom loving" group of radicals from the GOP because they purely object to government .Don't dare touch our light bulbs you"socialists" is the cry led by Michelle Backwards, Congresswoman.. elected THREE TIMES, eeeghgads?

Their leader in the Senate , Mitch McConnell proclaimed at the beginning of the first Senate session in 2008 that the Republican goal under his lofty residence as minority Senate leader would be to make Obama a one term president.

Surprisingly they have not objected as yet to all of the red stop lights in America affirming the legal obligation to stop your motor vehicle,and the green indicating an obligation to proceed. Such is their intelligence level.

Further many Republicans in the Senate have signed a non enforceable pledge fostered by a born to the cloth rich snob lobbyist,I refer to him as Grovel Nuttwist employed by publicly wealthy groups involved in politics to never raise taxes,a self serving aim if ever there was one. I also call him "Noogie"

There have been some who object to the obligation to pay an income tax. Fortunately they are in federal prison. The same "free spirits" are already in courts to obstruct the legal requirement to cover oneself with medical insurance so what else can we expect from these Neanderthals?

Automobile insurance has been a legal requirement for operating a motor vehicles in all states so this contremp is phony for reasons other than logic or intelligence.

LETTER TO GOVERNOR JAN BREWER, JAN. 14, 2011

It is ironic to see the word safety on the Arizona website.

There is no safety in your state from death by firearms Not for elected Federal representatives of tens of thousands of people , not for Presidentially appointed judicial officials or innocent 9 year old schoolchildren all of whom happen to be in a public place on a Saturday morning, enjoying their right of free assembly.

Sadly and Ironically Congresswoman Gabrielle Giffords was presumably "privileged " to read out the second amendment portion of the American Constitution in Congress a few days before her near assassination in Tucson, Arizona ,

Arizona is a beautiful but sorry State that has ~~free" open carry laws for firearms . Arizona seeths with hate for any number of reasons including the well known fact it is full of illegal aliens from Mexico who have inundated the area for decades and the population suffers from a high unemployment rate over ten percent but guns are as accessible (to the ill educated and even the undetected possibly drug addicted) as chewing gum or a pair of hedge clippers.

Representative Giffords, targeted for death by a poster goblin of insanity has publicly proclaimed ownership and ability to use a Glock automatic,ironically the type of gun she was mortally wounded with.The population wide ownership of guns of all description makes all citizens of Arizona an open target anytime and anyplace, restaurants, businesses ,taverns or church. That includes those who own and carry a weapon.

The patriotic rabble babble about our soldiers overseas making us safe or safer is so much propaganda by those corporate sponsored politicians PAC groups that would perpetuate our presence in over 400 overseas military installations throughout the world for their own profitable purposes. And for as long as possible. All while state,local and national laws permit easily concealed inexpensive weapons of mass murder available to just about anyone without permits or registration in many cases. All because Presidents who have been shot by the insane (Reagan) and Congresspersons who have lost part of their brains to bullets(See Tucson AZ Representative Giffords)favor the right to bear arms ! Insanity and illogic reigns.

Guns are universally more available than ever before due to the grotesque misinterpretation of the Constitution of the United States concerning the outdated armed "militias "by a small group of Republican appointed"Supreme Court justices "who apparently are in love with corporations including the one feared by most legislators of any party, the National Rifle Association whose sole avowed purpose is to render any law restricting guns of any kind impossible at any level. NRA purposes are to sell weapons that kill. Hunting animals is an afterthought ,automatics and armor piercing ammunition are a foremost selling feature. No animals wear armor.

The current interpretation of the 2nd Amendment pretends that almost any citizen has the right to bear arms even in the absence of any militia, such nineteenth century armed groups having fallen into disfavor or nonexistence over 150 years ago.

Every representative of the people of the United States of America has a duty to protect citizens and themselves against the mounting death toll of this maniacal liberalization of the freedom to bear arms. We are in danger of losing freedom from fear and civilization as we know it. Polls show the voters in our country would overwhelmingly welcome moves against the NRA and the terrible LIBERALS who have forced and finagled this madness on America, the previously Beautiful. And all for PROFIT!

I pity you having an Arizona legislature that would pass the gun laws now in effect in your state.

Sincerely,
Jack Doyle

HEADLINE;

AS THIS IS WRITTEN THE CARLISLE FUND IS BRINGING OUT A NEW IPO COVERING STOCKS IN THE TECHNOLOGY FIELD.

THIS FUND IS RUN BY SUCH AS THE CHENEY GROUP,GIULIANI AND FRIENDS,THE SAUDI FAMILIES INCLUDING THE PRINCE WHO GOT A 2 BILLION DOLLAR KICKBACK FROM BRITISH WAR PRODUCT MANUFACTURER BAE AND OF COURSE DADDY BUSH AND FRIENDS .

THERE ARE NOW ALIVE IN THIS COUNTRY INDIVIDUALS WHO "EARN" IN EXCESS OF ONE BILLION DOLLARS PER YEAR

THROUGH CONTROL OF THIS FUND OR FUNDS LIKE IT AND HEDGE FUNDS THAT ONLY ALLOW MILIONAIRES OR IN SOME CASES BILLIONAIRES TO INVEST WITH MINIMUM INVESTMENTS IN EXCESS OF HUNDREDS OF MILLIONS OF DOLLARS.

MANY PAY FIFTEEN PERCENT TAX (or less) ON THEIR INCOME DUE TO A TWISTED AND UNFAIR MANIPULATION OF THE TAX CODE BY REPUBLICANS IN A PREVIOUS CONGRESS.

YOU CAN ONLY IMAGINE HOW MUCH POWER AND INFLUENCE THIS WEALTH CAN EXERT IN GOVERNMENTS ALL OVER THE WORLD OF COURSE INCLUDING THE BEST GOVERNMENT CAN BUY, THE GOOD OLD U.S.A.

The leading R presidential candidate Romney earned somewhat less than 23 Million dollars in 2011 and upon examination was found to pay less than 14% in taxes, mostly "unearned" income.

Recently the President has sensibly and correctly demanded that changes be made in the tax code doing away with the unfairness of the "carried interest"rule that enables certain investors to pay far less percentages than earners (secretaries,ditch diggers,bus drivers,accountants,etc.) of far smaller sums .Republicans Boehner and others ,all leading candidates of GOP stripe claim this is the start of class warfare, laughable because it started with the Reagan Republican Administration and their change of the tax code way back 40 years ago when rates for the really wealthy were cut by over 40% and lower income wage earners were given a small income tax reduction but their social security rates were raised with no deductions allowed. Reagan and Senator Dollar Bill Bradley saved a small fortune every year ..and it has gotten worse and more unfair year after Republican Bush year. There is no waythe American budget can ever balance without new increases on those who large reap the largest sums of income,people and Corporations. PEOPLE,TAX PAYERS LIKE WARREN BUFFETT

AND BILL GATES AND THE MAJORITY OF TAXPAYERS IN THEIR CATEGORY KNOW THIS.

Why are the Republicans in Clowngress so ignorant or IDIOTIC?

MANY MONEY PUPPETS IN CONGRESS DANCE TO COMMANDS OF INDUSTRY

Wonder why the Democrats cannot control their own people in the Congress. Why is controlling the Dems like herding spastic cats?

How do the R folks get 100% votes against some plans that would benefit almost all the nations's population.? Because the citizens only vote once every four years and checks get written every day by Lobbyists and Capitalists sent to campaign funds of representatives in favor of opposing views

.It all comes down to money

Lobbyist make a living coming up with a pattern of half truths that can embrace negativity against things like making illegal immigrants who live in the United States into citizens or against Reformed Healthcare so that Democrats in Congress can become Republican in their opinions overnight when the check arrives and the lobbyist rings them up on the phone. Worse, most of the legal bribery is over a span of months and years and is epidemic and endemic.

Constant.

You can find out what organizations support anyone in Congress from the internet from organizations that keep track of this by the dollars and they report regularly on their findings.Many organizations are fronts for an industry group of groups.

But of course there are many things that take place without public scrutiny so perhaps for every dollar there is another one or two under the table . Or a free trip to Hawaii or Europe on a company plane and prepaid free hotel rooms, etc. You get the picture.

And the Supreme Court has allowed much of this as free speech?

In 1983 The Tax Reform of President Reagan and Democratic Senator "Dollar"Bill Bradley passed the Republican Congress with great fanfare changing the personal tax rate to two tiers, 25% and 15% .

Just in case you were interested both men profited handsomely with the new rates.

Conversely the rate on FICA increased with the purported reason that better have too much on hand rather than too little for later when payoff came. After all Social Security was " in trouble"

The FICA funds never were put aside however and the net result was more than 3 out of four working people were paying more into social security than into income taxes

The FICA funds went to make up for the egregious tax cuts for the wealthy and the manufacture of 24,000 atomic bombs - oh,great, glad they were put to good use!

LATER -2011 In more thoughtful times the Obama administration has taken 10,000 of these apart as Russia has reduced their arsenal as well. One little bump they may go off !

In the Bush 2007 budget our deficit showed a quarter of a trillion dollars less because FICA funds were used to keep the nation from nearly drowning but not quite..

BUSINESS "FRIENDS WITH BENEFITS" DO WELL UNDER REPUBLICANS

THE GOLDEN RULE-" THEM THAT HAS GETS!"
MORE !

While the general feeling now after bushs' bunch dispelled that Republican party principles bring overall prosperity for the country there are certainly well connected firms in manufacturing, service industries, and financial industry that have grown by leaps and bounds during GOP administrations. 2008 is overlooked by some, especially banks and some brokerages after Federal bailing out worked for them and not others.

Banking is American life's blood in business.

Modern day terminology refers to this as "friends with benefits".

The Carlyle fund with ex president (daddy)bush as an early investor and controlling figure and making investing decisions it is of course true that if the son of that ex president is president of the United States at the time there will be a direct connection that will benefit investments to be made by that Carlyle fund. Am I being suspicious ?

Of course this connection is not bravely displayed but it is in public view as much as it can be with a secretive administration and a secretively controlled Wall Street fund.

It is publicly known *Carlyle holds large percentages of ownership in Defense industries and has complete ownership of the largest earth moving firm in the world. That firm was developed and is in China which Communist state holds large amounts of US Treasury notes since America had to borrow heavily to finance escapades undertaken by the little bush in the White House during the past eight years. (such as the Iraq war, tax cuts for Oil companies and other wealthy supporters)and last but not least the infamous Bush tax cuts for the richest over a Trillion in deficits pending with no return except for their GOP Campaign coffers.

Carlyle is currently ready to enter the capital hungry banking industry * and going public in May 2012 but so far is precluded by law from doing so directly however they will press on with contacts in Congress and the Treasury department. Time will tell how eager the industry is for investment and how anxious the Obama administration is to accommodate both sides.

There are hundreds of obvious and even transparent similar situations but because our laws have been written in favor of such arrangements nothing is done to prevent them.

Just like the Supreme Court decision that allows industry backed interest groups to fund parties and candidates under the premise that such payment for advertising is "free speech" protected by the outdated but pre 1790 iconic constitution.. strangely in the history of the court with no laws or facts changing the dictum has evolved. (CONSERVATIVE?) ACTIVIST JUDGES?

The fact that an individual citizen cannot possibly buy up any percentage of the free speech that multi national industries with Billions in reserve are able to is not material to our newly discovered "law" and the fair and balanced"justices". And so it goes. "Them with the gold rules".!

Attitudes and prejudices of Justices appointed by a right leaning president bring harm to the general population who really have no control over 9 elderly persons in robes who have the job for "life".according to our archaic constipating laws.

At this point, a pertinent aside- I must bring up the NRA association with lobbyists in the White House and Congress on a daily basis during the past 8 years which explains why 30,000 people die every year due to laws that permit guns to be traded as easily as baseball cards and the easily hidden nature of the high capacity automatic weapon.

The NRA frightens many members of Congress because there are many states where a splinter group of hunter/sportsmen can swing an election although this is in reality exaggeration to a large degree .

Many sensible gun owner/hunters are not in favor of armor piercing bullets and automatic pistols or rifle/,machine guns, particularly when they can sold freely at gun shows to anyone with money and no background checks.

More than likely much of the drug cartel violence in Mexico is armed by smuggled weapons from America but this is vehmently denied by the NRA and their well financed incumbent Congressional and K Street Lobbyists. On that note the author wrote to retiring Congresswoman"Gabby" Gifford ------ see attached but no response will be forth-coming as taking on an entrenched NRA can be suicide for her future. And with the Billionaire financed established lob-bying industry against one it takes no imagination to believe anyone or many going against them can be anonymously "snuffed"easily with the wealth available and political futures at stake . Deniability is cheap and readily on call. What can 100 million dollars so famously flaunted recently in Nevada by a Gingrich supporter buy ? Just about anything except a decent winning candidate!

Remember even as shown in Vatican past murder can rule history.

As a recent example see the pattern of violence so well shown in the cinema about "Erin Brockovich" - the above statement is not a fiction of imagination. This may play out in the future and who will expose it? Iraq was a sick phony proposal and see how the media dealt with it gingerly at what devastating cost to America.

The Pentagon Papers of the NY Times Daniel Ellsburg 1971show what should have happened in the Iraq PHONY FAIRYTALE masquerade but didn't and why? A tortuous story of longtime deceit.

THE IRAQ INVASION AND WAR SCENARIO WAS A PERFECT HOAX, ALL DETAILS IN PLACE FOR A CHEERLEADER (bush) PAROXSYSM OF PATRIOTISM AND ACTION FIGURE SYMBOLISM WITH w. bush THE HERO! Manny Pulation of the Bush advertising department wrote the fictional contrived 'DOCUMENTARY".

"If you're not with us you are against us" the Bush PR man wrote and the action hero standing on the still smolder-ing pile of American capitalism and vaporized humanity defied any American journalist to question any of the falsi-fied details later supplied by peddlers of the Pentagon and Whitehouse and the constant lying never ending debacle it would lead to for DECADES TO COME. It was the Yale cheerleader's greatest moment!

Leading left leaning and middle of the road journalists became rangers of the right over the ramparts and into battle with ball point pen and word processor/compu-ter to "shock and AlQaeda, Saddam (they did not know each other) and Bin Laden(he was in a cave somewhere or secret safe house thousands of miles away from war,he hated Saddam Hussein) Reporters were embedded with troops, controlled neatly by armed service specialists -PR companions. Never before was any war so stage managed for presentation.

But Fox News and their "bench, and Rush Blimpo had fod-der for their cannon like mouths for a decade, war is always nice as a topic for the" news". The NY Post led the national propaganda effort making lies into fact and other newpa-pers followed the trend until much later when skepticism finally came into view, much TOO LATE!

IMAGINED HEADLINE-Could it happen?

Tea Party officials released plans today to name currently detained Jared Loughner as CEO of the organization.

Loughner's embracing of Orwellian thoughts and unique interpretations of grammar, semantics and arithmatic equations appeal to the Executive Board's plans for revamping American government and political institutions and will enable elected Tea Party individuals in Congress to present plans to the constituents who elected them and the assembled Congress that will quickly bring about a balanced budget. Further qualifying him as an ideal head of the organization is his ability like Martin Luther King to"dream" and he has many,he has pills for the purpose. .

Tea Party planners insist such ideas will be endorsed and supported by the FOX news agency that brands itself and is known as "FAIR AND BALANCED."

As an example board members referred to Jared's well known plan for interpreting numbers as, for instance, the number six as 18 and interpreting words(using the Lewis Carroll"Alice in Wonderland"concept) as the speaker says they mean.This follows the famous W Bush" signing statement "practice of the former administration which set a frequency record of changing the meaning of any law passed by the US Congress to whatever the Imperial Executive needed it to say or mean.

Furthermore Loughner's use of multifaceted firearms and his practiced use will appeal to members across a broad spectrum of believers in "second amendment remedies" when election tallies do not match with announced Tea Party candidates

The Tea Party has appealed to members and NRA members for donations toward Jared's anticipated "bothersome" (their term) bail and legal expenses .On line and

TV Testimonials by Loughner for GLOCK Corp. products are planned upon his release. F. Lee Bailey ,who recently discovered" OJ "is innocent will be expected to head up a group of respected lawyers eagerly waiting to file papers to enable this future Tea Party Icon the freedom that the recently reborn American Constitution has guaranteed believers since it was written.

Taxpayers will be paying expenses for both defense and prosecution. Since most taxpayers are not members of this group Teapartiers interviewed expressed relief at being unburdened for such an extraordinary expense and thankful for this "FREEDOM" from the taxes the group condemns .

The group expects to be included in the two NATIONAL RIFLE ASSOCIATION gatherings to be held in Arizona this month where some hunters and real gunners (owners of automatics) by the thousands are expected. Celebrations at these events approving the finding of not guilty in the trial of a sponsor of the gun show where an eight year old boy was allowed and encouraged to fire an automatic carbine with which he accidently shot himself dead. The NRA approves this message and invites all to future assemblies. Body armor is suggested.

GUNS ARE UNIVERSALLY AVAILABLE NOW and are legal only recently because of the grotesque misinterpretation of the Constitution of the United States concerning the outdated useless armed "militias "by a small group of Republican appointed"Supreme Court justices "who apparently are in love with corporations including the one feared by most legislators of any party, the National Rifle Association whose sole avowed purpose is to render any law restricting guns of any kind impossible at any level. NRA purposes are not for hunting guns but for selling weapons that kill.

The current interpretation of the 2nd Amendment pretends that almost any citizen has the right to bear arms even in the absence of any militia,such neanderthal armed groups having fallen into disfavor or nonexistence over 150 years ago.

Every representative of the people of the United States of America has a duty to protect citizens and themselves against the mounting death toll of this maniacal liberalization of the freedom to bear arms.We are in danger of losing freedom from fear and civilization as we know it. Polls show the public would overwhelmingly welcome moves against the NRA and the terrible LIBERALS who have forced and finagled this madness on America,the previously Beautiful.

MANY TIMES WE SEE COMMENTS BY THINK TANKS INTRUDING ON GOVERNMENT in

newspaper quotes,

THE CATO INSTITUTE first founded as the Koch Institute. The Koch Brothers front organization for "libertarian ideas"meaning whatever they say it means cause they have so much money and have bought so much influence in Washington, DC meaning the people we elect,",Clowngressman and Servitudonors better toe the line and believe!

Another " thinktank" we see often in print is the Heritage Foundation, the internet Homepage of which shows like mounted stuffed Elks the faces of Rush Limpo and Shawn Hennessy, BLAZONING THEIR BOAST OF 700,000 members. And for twenty five bucks they will make YOU a member,send you a copy of the US outdated antique Constitution and a book written by one of their overstuffed self important leaders propagandizing a favorite theme of the GREED based organization.

Of the two "Think tanks" the first CATO seems more confused since they purport to be against both Republicans and Democrats ,at times in favor of them both, which for their purposes covers the need for influence with all decision makers. Hence Libertarians?

I mention the two groups because they are insidious underhanded associations of very wealthy corporations and individuals who have for the past forty years sought to control the country while pretending to be "friends of the court" bringing so called independent research to questions that affect their powerful members biasing results toward their monetary interests. They work closely with lobbyists. One major aim has been to destroy the influence of labor unions. Their efforts have been terminally destructive to American workers.

For further illustration look for the Documentary film "HEIST"about how a tobacco lawyer named Lewis Powell became a Supreme Court justice and began a move to"protect"the Free Enterprise system by favoring the treatment of corporations in decisions before the court as individuals and enabling money to be given by them to candidates and causes. His confidential memo to the US Chamber of Commerce started corporate advocacy groups and his arguments in court during 1978 were the evil seed of Corporate Donations unlimited that are now the cause of massive money manipulation of elections.

In America Union members have dwindled from one in three to one in fourteen. Efforts by the Republican Governor and legislature in Wisconsin since the 2010 election are a typical example. The weakening of unions has put less spendable income in the hands of middle class families to keep the wheels of commerce turning. So we have come upon the ratio of the one percent and 99% or at best the 90% at the lower level and ten percent on the mountain. Whichever, this income distribution is a destructive non starter for the American economy. There is no longer the American dream ,typical June Cleaver Mom at home while Dad works one job that pays enough to cover the mortgage ,food ,clothes ,retirement ,etc. and this has become our disaster! We have met the enemy and he is us and who the hell elected him?

What is puzzling is the long period of time it has taken to realize this poisonous self defeating mechanism and why the captains of industry in their CHAMBERS OF COMMERCE and INDUSTRIAL ASSOCIATIONS have not seen for themselves that businesses depend on large numbers and the rapid flow through or velocity of money for commerce to thrive. They have killed the golden goose.They need the 99% and spending. People like Warren Buffett,Bill Gates know this but Republican politicians are oblivous to it .As are hard core Boards of Directors,owners and CEO's.

The House just passed a tax cut for the owners of small business (up to 600 employees) of 20% allowing them to spend it as they please, wanna bet it does nothing to create jobs if it gets through? It enriches the wealthiest in the nation and adds to the deficit 47 Billion dollars. Tax cuts ,Elections.! This is the GOP!

August 10,2011

Senator Robert Menedez

US Senate 528 Hart Office Bldg

Washington,D.C. 20510

Dear Senator Menendez,

As my representative you should know I have great contempt for the"compromise" just forced on the people of the United States by a small cult representing only 15% of America forced on Congress by Fox news Dick Armey and others I detest. Non fanatic citizens are being disenfranchised by legalisms that should not exist in the United States Congress.

The forthcoming appointed "twelve wisemen" will be prevented from doing the right thing by taxing the super wealthy corporations and individuals some even richer than corporations. The political dozen will come up with road kill in their much publicized negotiations. So the forced sword of economic Damocles will render devastating "deficit reduction" in all the wrong areas harmful to Americans as did the useless debt ceiling contrivance that hung around for 90 years accomplishing less than nothing.

The worst wasted expense this country has endured for 60 years is the defense budget We lost in Korea ,Vietnam, Lebanon, Iraq and Afghanistan. Wasted money equal to all expenditures by all the countries in the world with casualties and civilian deaths exceeding hundreds of thousands against third world nations having no air force ,navy, tanks, electronics industry ,radar guided missile and yet we are in the middle of ten useless years supposedly "protecting our homeland." Our presence in the middle east invites the Insane to do pointless mayhem on us and their own people and continues to do so with no value whatsoever to either side. Our planning has transported targets over to the jihadists at great financial and human cost accomplishing nothing.

We are slaves to Republican Military Industrialist propaganda .Please end the waste of lives and fortune.

Certainly you know there are hundreds of expenses that can be reduced before Social Security and, Medicare which have been paid for over decades by citizens who are entitled to them .....Hence, "Entitlements".

Furthermore the crisis created by the Republican House of Representatives and their cult like robots is likely to ruin the economy of the United States and the world .It is not created by compromise , only by Machiavellians seeking power none of whom are Democrats and polls show the voters know this -Democrats should act accordingly.

Sincerely,

Jack Doyle

INTERJECTION 2012

I am pleased to add to this letter (which is no doubt similar to thousands sent to Clowngress) that an a year EARLIER departure from Iraq and Afghanistan has been announced by President Obama as of 2011-2012.

THE BUSH TAX RATE RAPE

There are still people in places of power and responsibility who pretend the tax cuts bush gave to the wealthiest of earners in 2002 were beneficial to the people of America but the proof of additional jobs since year 2000 to2010 is nonexistent and a raging depression and ten % unemployment is glaring proof of the fiction of this rape of the middle class. When ten percent of the population has 90%of the wealth and billionaire Warren Buffett's secretary pays a higher tax rate than he does and he comments famously on that fact we know sham and shame is abounding in our tax code while mendacity and deceit is uppermost in tax "planners"designs.

May I point out that even after this evidence so called" authorities" like Republican Rep Paul Ryan want to lower tax rates not only for the wealthy but for corporations while adding another burden to the middle class in the form of a "Value Added taxof8% while making medicare more expensive for the poor and elderly.

Republican cheerleaders for front groups like the Heritage Foundation and the Cato Institute are already waging blogging warfare where it will put their nefarious plans before the public as a new way to get the US out of deficit .It's sick but happening.

DYING BREED – DUSTY REPUBLICAN REMAINS FROM A DISTANT PAST.

Those names that have been mentioned as potential contenders for the GOP presidential hopeless , in 2010 are sputtering out in ridiculous fashion with Sarah Palin proud of her dancing (newly a mother)daughter ditched before getting to the alter and the "fishing shack fiancé" authoring articles about Mama Palin(a firm believer in abstinence) having allowed the two young lovers to sleep together in the Palin household in plain sight.

It was a hypocritical spectacle during the Palin introduction appearance on stage with the entire family as a keynote of McCain's campaign.

All it lacked was Daddy Palin's sled dogs to make it the perfect faux American Values family portrait in spite of the unintended pregnancy as R devotees gushed about how every family has problems etc.

Gee John just not on stage with a baby and a band! And flags waving….

.And now comes the truth from some of the cast of unbelievable characters. Just like the books written about little boy bush by none other than his press secretary, Scott

McClellan, another written by his Sec. Of the Treasury Paul O'Neill-and yet another written by his appointed Security Advisor, Richard Clarke - the truth will out as they say and there is little that can be said to refute the facts as presented by those who were there in the thick of things.

Clarke's writings were painfully misrepresented by the Repub faithful and appointees like Connie (cover W's ass) Rice . Clarke was very pointed in bringing the administrations failings to the forefront. Lie after lie was told by the history rewriters about his efforts to bring Al Quada into view as a threat to no avail.

We must also point out another embarrassing presidential hopeful, Sen. John Ensign who after denials apologized to his Senate colleagues for his sexcapades with a friendly paid aide,very friendly. He also paid her cuckolded husband during the long period of months when he was sharing the same woman and getting him and her to do political chores while the female half of the hired team satisfied his sexual desires. Both were paid out of an orfice fund.?, Talk about multitasking.

Another of the family values team,the vanishing governor of South Carolina also was mentioned as a potential president under the Gas and Oil Party banner but his recent disappearing act along the way with no one able to explain his location on Father's day leaving his wife and four kids behind for 5 days labels him a flake and phony as well since a trip to Argentina would seem to indicate activities along the lines of Sen. Ensign..

Sanford's explanation seemed to indicate he was hiking. Hiking,? This is hard to believe especially when he told no one including his family where he was going and he ditched his security guards deliberately.

Take a hike gov!

NEWSFLASH, the internet and TV just showed the absent governor's admission to an affair with a chiquita in Argentina,, a ten second span from when the above sentence was typed on the word processor. The governor contrite in the first public admission of his dalliance said he was a "man of faith". Just not a faithfulman?There's one of Newt's excuses,good old forgiving GOD again. Handy for Republican trysts.

Oh well, there's still Newt! Ask him how he handles medical insurance when cancer strikes his family.

SOME of his former wives can detail that sick affair-Seems these important people in the R party treat their women just like men do in Iran, Iraq or Saudi Arabia ,like barnyard animals.

Thinking back, did you ever see a photo of Pat Nixon smiling?

The party of Family Values is holding firm to the hypocrites oath, " do as I say - notice not what I do."

DISGUSED BRIBES ,ENTIRE CONGRESS BOUGHT OFF DURING "CONTRACT ON AMERICA"ERA

Back in "the Day"Newt Getrich received an advance on a book that had not even been written or titled from a division of Fox News,owned by Australian far right Rupert Murdoch -,Dirty Daddy Warbucks .

At that time foreign companies were forbidden to own newpapers or communications firms in a market where they had a TV or radio network presence.

Strange to say an educated person like Newt had not even known the ownership by Murdoch of the company passing the disguised bribe however he was already preparing an override in Congress of the rules that prevented such mass media control of a segment of the communications industry.

Without boring the reader with the details of this control coup the override went swimmingly with massive Republican support in Congress which at the time controlled by the GAS &OIL PARTY (GOP) it could not be vetoed by Clinton.

So from the time the Fox News Network worked to become the mouthpiece of the Republican Party with Roger Ailes of the Reagan Administration taking charge of the whole company after his"service" to the country in the Gipper's regime.

Newt of course wrote his book, and made SUBSTANTIAL money on the publication of same as it became a suggested book for all R's who were enthralled by the boy genius with no morals, scruples or truth in him, all as he served as Speaker of the House for the US government and served the red necked State of Georgia who strongly supported him but turned down Max Cleland who lost three limbs from a hand grenade blast serving his country. Cleland was a victim of a slime campaign against him that reached disgusting proportions, the GOP was desperate for that seat.

So a War hero was rejected for self serving Newt. Thanks to the American Idiots,voters of the Clay based state ,Georgia.

That of course reflects heavily on the intellect of the citizens and voters of the Peach State that has supported R party candidates since they started pushing wars and corruption as a general policy because so much industry in the State depends on war, any war as long as it used Georgia products and not peaches but electronics,communication systems, such firms as Lockheed and Martin as examples. Talk about idols with feet of clay.

Cleland was not the only victim of Republican cesspool tricks, even John McCain was victimized in the primary with him against the lying incompetent George H.W.Bush who ultimately was "awarded" the election by a "Supreme" court Justice appointed by his father, the most contested and disastrous presidency in the history of the nation.

McCain was accused of having had an illegal Negro child during the South Carolina campaign which disturbed the bigoted voters in the R base in the State enough to swing the selection to '"W" .McCain and his wife had adopted the black child years prior from Bangladesh.

Recently the Obama Whitehouse has labeled the Fox "news" network as biased and untrustworthy for good reason. They headline commentators who speak out complete insults of Obama personally"calling him a racist" accusing executives in the adminstration of being communists and the like. The list goes on.

The problem lies with lies and liars such as Glen Beck, Bill O'Reilley, Hannety and lesser lights liars.

This is a Nazi tactic of the'BIG LIE" adopted by Joseph Goebbels ,Hitler's propaganda minister-tell the same untruth often enough and it soon is believed by captive listeners.

Fox,to give them credit has captured viewers by having a quality lineup of talented producers of entertainment,Glee,American Idol, TV drama"House" sit-coms and others,these lead viewers to their Faux News programs which they claim are "fair and balanced" but independent observers know otherwise.

IDIOTS PASS GAS IN THE NIGHT

Sorry, but that's the most appropriate name for people like Mike Pence(Congressman from Indiana) Dick Armey(thrown out of his job and party function) and Newt Getrich.

(don't have to tell you who he is since he emanates disgusting vibes clear across America).

They lead or encouraged a group of sickos who marched on Washington DC protesting big government,,taxes and President Obama who was elected obviously by someone other than them.

Nazi tactics like the Putsch in Munich were evident (forget about the rendering, tapping of phones and torture) just to ad to the festivities for the week end.

Young children carried signs accusing the PRESIDENT of being a socialist, a communist and all were bussed in, who paid for the busses?Read up on it. It was a disgusting episode in American history.Fox ``News" loved showing the spectacle .

If those creeps and uglies represented America it's a good time to become Canadian or Australian.

SO WE HAVE BUDGETS FOR THE RICH AND ANOTHER ONE FOR THE REST OF US.?WHICH ONE WILL THE FOUNTAIN BLESS? A FAMOUS REPUBLICAN ICON of strength, common sense,duck hunting,bourbon and straight talk said

"'DEFICITS DON'T MATTER'' and that 's the way the Gas and Oil party rolled until 2008 when just enough hicks from the sticks got angry about it and said we're not gonna take it anymore. Sadly for them it's too late to get fiscal religion since the cost of the previous burden is going to make it impossible to push the boulder uphill without massive new income taxes and spending cuts as well.....The major problem is most Republicans like Dick Cheney are obscenely wealthy as the result of easily gathered money from the military industrialist (read Oil/'Gas)complex made large by manipulating tax laws AS A GROUP while they were in power..

This money is not the result of mind /life improving invention such as the wealth of Bill Gates but is a result of connivance and legal deceit,arranging to be in the right place at the right time usually through an election or by insider trading in the stock market and both.These kind of people do not think of donating half of their fortunes to a good cause as Gates ,Warren Buffett and others are doing.THEY ARE THE GREEDY NEEDY SEEDY CLASS who aim for political dominance ad infinitum.

Therefore the rich upper ten percent of our earning population do not want any tax placed on what they have, rich people will prefer and secretly finance a VALUE ADDED TAX that will fall more heavily on the middle class and poor who will absorb more than 80% of the levy since there are numerically more of them .England depends heavily on VAT as does much of Europe and they are more heavily taxed than taxpayers in America.

Obviously as will be seen Rep .Paul Ryan is the ADVANCE MAN FLAGWAVER for this new way for America ,the wealthy to avoid diminishing their accumulated fortunes. His plan" for the future" cuts the top tax rate for the already wealthy and CORPORATIONS AS WELL from 35% to25%.

Sound fair and equitable to you? This will not fly In American politics since in addition to the onerous and unfair tax schemes it floats it includes the end of Medicare and Ryan's plan will include messing with Social Security as well secretively! Meanwhile, the oil industry is not using its profits to hire more people.

Senator   Paul recently falsely claimed the oil companies employ 9.2 million people — in fact, there are only 2.2 million jobs in the entire oil industry, and 40 percent of those jobs are minimum-wage work at gas stations. Exxon Mobil, Chevron, Shell, and BP have shed their U.S. workforce by 11,200 between 2005 to 2010, according to a report last year. Big Oil isn't investing in renewable energy or in reducing oil spills, either.

Strangely, while Kyl and Paul called an end to oil subsidies indefensible, they used the opportunity to label clean energy tax credits "crony government." During his clean energy rant, Paul said:

"It doesn't seem right that your tax dollars are sent to companies just because they're big contributors." This from a man who got over $100,000. From the oil industry. Seems solar and wind are not paying him off! And who said young people like him? They should stick to HipHop moguls.

Republicans have received 88 percent of donations from the oil industry's coffers. In the Senate, Republicans have taken over $13.8 million from oil, compared to the Democrats' $3.3 million, meaning Senate Republicans have taken four times the amount in Big Oil contributions as Democrats. Kyl is the No. 29 largest recipient in the Senate from oil and gas in career contributions with over $330,000 and Paul has received over $106,000 from oil.

A VIRTUAL TORRENT OF WHAT EVIL LURKS .

Every time there seems to be a finale to this book pending another subject arises that indicates the ignorance and venality that abounds in America.

The unbalanced twit Sharon Angle that ran for Senator in Nevada against Harry Reid (who in my opinion is no prize) in the poorly educated thinly populated state has embraced the Pee party arguments against the IRS, the Departments of Education , and other governmental essential agencies to win the Republican nomination and now brings real guns,BANG BANG to the fight with the statement that if she does not win the election it should be settled by citizens `` gathering up their guns and exercising the right to bear arms against a government they cannot trust" because the electorate did not see fit to install her as their Senator. Armed insurrection? This in a campaign speech? Unbelievable.

She really deserved a jail term but anything goes when it is undertaken by a right wing zealot IN THE WITLESS WEST.

This convoluted revolutionary notion is typical of the thought process of this weird splinter group that so desperately seeks power. But it seems to be an advance warning of the paranoia of someone who is certifiably dangerous to all exposed to her and her future planning ,something like the mentally deficient group of 7 or 8 "militiamen" self labeled "Hutaree" who planned to kill law enforcement officials in Indiana who mounted a defense they were only defending themselves.(against what should be asked) Their headquarters was a discarded trailer with no wheels.

DISGUSTINGLY, OUR SOFT HEADED INDIANA JUSTICE SYSTEM FOUND THEM NOT GUILTY. Another plan later "boys" ,bite of the apple? Taxpayers paid for the defense. Since police were the target they may be under surveillance for a little while we sincerely hope.

It is somewhat(not totally) reassuring that those who would do harm to "normal" Americans who go to places of worships like church,school and work every day with a plan to live a moral and normal life are so ignorant for the most part that they tip their abnormality to authorities in advance by totally insane actions.

Some publicized actions by TERRORISTS (BY NO MEANS ALL OF THEM) INCLUDE; trying to drive into the US from Canada with a trunk load of dynamite with plans to blow up Los Angeles airport. And attempting to get a refund on an exploded rental truck used to implode the parking garage of the WTC resulting in the arrest of the entire group of hatred infected Muslims that participated including the bloodthirsty "Imam" leading the plot. And oh yes ,another dedicated jihadist was caught singlehandedly trying to cut down the Brooklyn Bridge by attacking one support strand with a power saw in broad daylight. ,recently there was also a plan to attack the military installation of Fort Dix ,NJ populated with thousand of armed MP's and sentinels of the US Army by a few dedicated bearded Muslims who had a pizza delivery truck and a few handguns. The plan was to kill American soldiers..! Please allow me to Include Sharon Angle - non muslim among them except she is supposed to be American ,one of"us" .Lucky even some R's including the Republican mayor of Reno considered this flaky woman dangerous and too far right and vowed to campaign for Democrat Reade.. The fact that Harry Reid is powerful as leader of the Senate and has seniority that any Representativewould wait a decade for is important to the well being and future of Nevada. As November arrived the importance of Reid carried him as an incumbent winner .

Does it not seem Sharon Angle has indicated she ranks with such as those seeking to harm our nation with armed insurrection ? Gabriel Gifford, Congresswoman shot by loony gun nut Jared Loughner may have been an unsuspecting suggested target by this self promoting Angle, a twisted first amendment fanatic. Those who supported Angle need careful examination of their motives and purposes and should be kept out of politics for the good of the nation.

CONSERVATIVES LIKE BAGS OF MANURE FOR SALE IN OPPOSITION TO UNIONS

Recently the ACU (American Conservative Union), one of the largest "conservative" organizations in the United States sent a letter to transportation company FEDEX soliciting a contract for three million or more dollars to join the firm in pissing on their Union in several ways including contacting 150,000 people at least seven times each. The ACU is staffed by none other than a former deputy Labor secretary in the Reagan Administration (no doubt he was pro labor?) who wrote the letter asking for the money and outlining the scheme.

When FEDEX turned down the offer for unknown reasons (is it possible they thought it a rotten idea ?) the chairman of ACU wrote a letter to United Parcel offering basically the same services.

When the manure hit the fan in the newspapers (thanks for a FREE PRESS) the chairman denied he was offering the support of the ACU organization and said he was simply proposing under his own aegis although the letter was WRITTEN ON ACU STATIONERY which also had the emblem of several other "conservative" lobbies;

Calling this group weasels and skunks is insulting to wild life .But then I suppose they think they are conserving "values" for profit hungry investors.

Yakoff Smirnoff was right, "WHAT A COUNTRY".

General Petraeus RETIRED IN August 2011 appointed to head the CIA .Will he cheerlead an Iran war?

The military man who convinced college cheerleader bush to add troops in Iraq should have been named Betrayus since now years after that move our men or Iraqi citizens still die in bunches or one at a time in a land that has no protection or peace even as we leave them to their Iraqi inspired decisions and devices. Another name for him would have been Persuadus since Obama was suckered into adding 30,000 more fighters to the conflict in Afghgoinonagain with similar wasteful results as of 2012..

Obama continues to follow "Boots on the ground" advise during these wars following Republican demands for continued presence in the two countries that lead us to military and fiscal purgatory. I hope and it appears our desperate decision on the deficit ceiling will force a final decision to leave this never ending fiasco much sooner than 2014.

It was revealed 18 Billion in 100 dollar bills bundled up, .shrink wrapped and shipped in C130 transports to Iraq helped hold down on violence between Sunnis and Bathes ,distributed by mullahs and tribal chieftans to their relatives,aides and loyalists.But still to be solved problems continue in that screwed up country. A US government investigation now reveals a total of 60 Billion totally wasted ,So called mercenaries cost us plenty and over 2000 of them died from insurgent actions.

These fortunes have been wasted in Afghoinongagain, all unaudited and under no control by the US Federal Reserve. In June this year news reporters could get no accounting of these billions of taxpayer dollars sent to gang leaders in 2 hellhole countries America should have left 8 years ago......

It seems no one wants to remember the advices of those veteran military analysts who decreed openly and constantly from the start that TRIPLE the amount of troops would be required to "WIN"and maintain a peace in the poverty stricken religiously torn countries even if decisive victories were won (which happened then in Afghanistan and then unhappened). Kabul as of early 2012 is still a ticking truckload of dynamite ready to kill Americans and Afghans alike all at once to no purpose.

Republican war whore cheer leaders in the media and of course Generals still in service maintain the "surges" have accomplished a normalcy in the two war theaters but orders were given to American commanders in the area to stay safe behind the walls of "forts" when the buildup occurred in Iraq leaving them to keep control of their nation holding American casualties down considerably.

But we continue to lose lives limbs and a fortune in both countries. After all how can any of our military anticipate that a quarter of a million American troops can take over a land where there are a potential one billion and a half potential religious zealots taught to hate us. Such exceptional ignorance on our part!!!

And The Worst Yet, time and again Iraq and Afghanistan uniformed personnel turn their weapons on our men who die betrayed by the very people they are "helping secure peace". How can our soldiers trust such so called allies? Do you want your family members in that job? American troops are now guarding each other in sleep in turns.. Car Bombs and Afghan soldiers killing American troops are a frequent occurrence as of May 2012.

If Obama's girls were there or Mitt Robme's boys were in uniform there the war would be over quickly.

Wilkopeida statistics show the costs of the War on Terror are often contested since many In Congress and politicians, lobbyists etc.have their share of blame and want to shed or hide it as academics and critics of the component wars (including the Iraq War) have unearthed many hidden costs not represented in official estimates. The most recent major report on these costs come from Brown University in the form of the Costs of War project,[1] which said the total for wars in Iraq, Afghanistan, and Pakistan is at least $3.2-4 trillion.[2] The report disavowed previous estimates of the Iraq War's cost as being under $1 trillion, saying the Department of Defense's direct spending on Iraq totaled at least $757.8 billion, but also highlighting the complementary costs at home, such as interest paid on the funds borrowed to finance the wars and a potential nearly $1 trillion in extra spending to care for veterans returning from combat through 2050.[3]

Those figures are significantly more than typical estimates published just prior to the start of the Iraq War, many of which were based on a shorter term of involvement. For example, in a March 16, 2003 *Meet the Press* interview of Vice President Dick Cheney, held less than a week before the Iraq War began, host Tim Russert reported that "every analysis said this war itself would cost about $80 billion, recovery of Baghdad, perhaps of Iraq, about $10 billion per year. We should expect as American citizens that this would cost at least $100 billion for a two-year involvement.".[4] US = US SUCKERS.

CONTINUING THE Afghanistan cost of war –CHECK BACK TO; October 05, 2010 "Kabul Press" - -- The 1984 emulating Pentagon will not tell the public what it costs to locate, target and kill a single Taliban soldier because the price-tag is so scandalously high that it makes the Taliban appear to be Super-Soldiers instead of zealots in sandals,robes and Toyota trucks. As set out in this article, the estimated cost to kill each Taliban is as high as $100 million, with a conservative estimate being $50 million. A public discussion should be taking place in the United States regarding whether the Taliban have become too expensive an enemy to defeat.

Each month the Pentagon generates a ream of dubious statistics designed to create the illusion of progress in Afghanistan. In response this author decided to compile his own statistics. As the goal of any war is to kill the enemy, the idea was to calculate what it actually costs to kill just one of the enemy. The obstacles encountered in generating such a statistic are formidable. The problem is that the Pentagon continues to illegally classify all negative war news and embarrassing information. Regardless, some information has been collected from independent sources. Here is what we know in summary and round numbers:

1. Taliban Field Strength: 35,000 troops

2. Taliban Killed Per Year by Coalition forces: 2,000 (best available information)

3. Pentagon Direct Costs for Afghan War for 2010: $100 billion

4. Pentagon Indirect Costs for Afghan War for 2010: $100 billion

Using the fact that 2,000 Taliban are being killed each year and that the Pentagon spends $200 billion per year on the war in Afghanistan, one simply has to divide one number into the other. That calculation reveals that $100 million is being spent to kill each Taliban soldier. In order to be conservative, the author decided to double the number of Taliban being killed each year by U.S. and NATO forces (although the likelihood of such being true is unlikely). This reduces the cost to kill each Taliban to $50 million, which is the title of this article. The final number is outrageously high regardless of how one calculates it.

To put this information another way, using the conservative estimate of $50 million to kill each Taliban: Existing estimate of hardcore devoted Taliban troops with no reinforcements 35,000 in war zone.

It costs the American taxpayers $1 billion to kill 20 Taliban Extrapolating the figures   JUST KILLING EXISTING TALIBAN WOULD COST $1.75 TRILLION AND SEVENTEEN YEARS @2000 DT PER YEAR .

And the 9% approval rating Republicans in Congress want to continues such travesty cutting spending on American healthcare of all kinds and foodstamps .VOTERS AND DEAR GODS,REPLACE CONGRESSIONAL REPUBLICANS PLEASE.

DYING BREED - THE REPUBLICAN REMAINS FROM A DISTANT GRAND PAST.

Those names that have been mentioned as potential contenders for the R presidential hopeless , hopefuls in 2010 are sputtering out in ridiculous fashion with Sarah Palin having her pregnant no more daughter ditched before getting to the alter and the "fishing shack fiancé" authoring articles about Mama Palin(a firm believer in abstinence) having allowed the two young lovers to sleep together in the Palin household in plain sight, according to the departing hockey lover/star.

The 2008 Palin opening appearance on stage with the entire family during the McCain campaign lacked just Daddy Palin's sled dogs to make it the perfect hypocritical American Values family portrait in spite of the unintended pregnancy (as Repub cheerleaders gushed about how every family has problems, etc)..And now comes the truth from one of the cast of unbelievable characters. Just like the book written about little boy bush (W for war whore) by none other than his press secretary, Scott McClellan-another written by his Sec. Of the Treasury Paul O'Neill-and yet another written by his CIA Appointee and Ambassdor and advisor Joe Wilson------ the truth will out as they say and there is little that can be said to refute the published facts.

We should also point out a formerly presidential hopeful, Sen. John Ensign who just apologized to his Senate colleagues for his long term sexual exploits with a friendly paid aid (he also paid the cuckolded husband)during the long period of months when he was sharing the same woman and getting him and her to do political chores while the female half of the multi tasked and satisfied his sexual desires. Were they paid out of an orfice fund.. Or Office fun? Maybe A funny fund?

The REPUB vanishing governor of Tenn. also was mentioned as a potential bidder for president under the Gas and Oil Party banner but his recent disappearing act along the way with no one able to explain his location on Father's day leaving his wife and four kids behind for 5 days labels him a flake and phony as well since a trip to Argentina would seem to indicate activities along the lines of Sen. Ensign .

Sanford's explanation indicated he was hiking .Hiking,? This is hard to believe especially when he told no one including his family where he was going and he ditched his security guards deliberately.

Take a hike gov!

FLASH One minute after the preceding sentence was entered on the word processor the very contrite Governor of Dolly Parton's state admitted publicly on TV that he was having an affair, I kid you not, no one told me I just gave it a sure guess.

And in his statement he said he was a man of "faith". Another "conservative exposed".

Oh well, there's still Noot! Ask him how he treats cancer when it strikes his family.

That is a sick story that we should all know indicative of the heartless attitudes of some.

It is interesting to see how so many important Republicans seem to treat their women as barnyard animals. Like Saudi Arabia,Iraq ,Iran or anywhere in the middle east.Did you ever catch Patricia Nixon in a photo smiling?

Another interesting facet of Repug guys caught in very embarrassing situations is their suddenly deep abiding faith in the lord.(See Colson going to Prison after Watergate conviction and becoming a minister) And Noot finding faith in the Catholic Church - it denotes they will accept anyone. Bring money.

Google up how many of them have become born again!

Internet observations:

So it's come down to this. On Saturday, **David Stockman**, the legendary Reagan budget chief who presided over the Reagan supply-side tax cuts, announced that the "debt explosion has resulted not from big spending by the Democrats, but instead the Republican Party's embrace, about three decades ago, of the insidious doctrine that deficits don't matter if they result from tax cuts." The next day, the former Fed chairman **Alan Greenspan**, who famously **helped sell the 2001 Bush tax cuts** to Congress, declared them simply "disastrous." Thanks for nothing "genius".

Sadly, Stockman and Greenspan are just about the only voices in the Republican Party speaking the truth about the fiscal devastation wrought by **the expiring Bush tax cuts**. After all, the **national debt** tripled under Ronald Reagan, only to double again during the tenure of George W. Bush. And as it turns out, the **Bush tax cut windfall** for the wealthy **accounted for almost half the budget deficits** during his presidency and, **if made permanent**, would contribute more to the U.S. budget deficit than the Obama stimulus, the TARP program, the wars in Afghanistan and Iraq, and revenue lost to the recession - *combined*. Of course, you'd never know it listening to the leaders of GOP.

And that's just the beginning. Here, then, are 10 Republican Lies about the Bush tax cuts:

117

- **Lie #1: Democrats Plan Across the Board Tax Hikes on January 1st**

- **Lie #2: Democrats Want a $3.8 Trillion Tax Increase**

- **Lie #3: Tax Cuts Pay for Themselves**

- **Lie #4: The Bush Tax Cuts Didn't Add to the Deficit**

- **Lie #5: Expiring High Income Tax Cuts Will Hurt Small Business**

- **Lie #6: The Estate Tax Devastates Small Businesses and Family Farms**

- **Lie #7: The Bush Tax Cuts Helped All Americans**

- **Lie #8. Extending Bush Tax Cuts for the Wealthy is the Best Way to Stimulate the Economy**

- **Lie #9. Bush Tax Cuts Produced 52 Straight Months of Job Growth**

Lie #1: Democrats Plan Across the Board Tax Hikes on January 1st

On July 19, Michigan Republican **Dave Camp** sent out an email blast warning of the "Democrats' ticking tax time bomb" claiming "Americans to pay higher taxes starting January 1, 2011." On July 20, Rep. **Mike Pence**(R-IN) declared, "Should Democrats get their way, every income tax bracket will increase on Jan. 1, 2011. Every single one."

It's no wonder **Politifact** deemed the charge "False." As the fact checking site put it:

"For many months, Democratic officials have consistently said that they intend to let only the tax cuts for the wealthiest individuals expire.

Due to the Peeparty influence on the antique debt ceiling debate we should have been so lucky.Obama bargained by continuing this cut for another 2 years to gain extended unemployment benefits and an end to the debate about the debt ceiling.

OBVIOUSLY DISHONEST POLITICIANS THRIVE DURING DEPERATE TIMES THEY CREATED

The ex Vice president of America, The aptly name Dick Cheney is a perfect example and of course there are dozens walking free as citizens under no legal cloud while others plot to do exactly the same wrongs as many , elected and appointed, have in the past.

Dick is proud of his insistence on entering a war in Iraqnam while neglecting to secure or finish the war in Afghanistan.

Dick who(famously said "deficits don't matter") enriched himself by multimillions of dollars as part owner and President of Halliburton while in the post. Even after - while vice president - as Halliburton profited in Iraq and other government contracts,he is the richest ex VP in history. His "separation " from the company included future profits that were sure to accrue because of the fiasco he induced in Iraqnam for position in the oil fields.He didn't fight to the Supreme Court to keep his conversations with the oil executives secret because they were about the weather.

.In the past the Vice Presidential post was evaluated by one as "not worth a warm bucket of spit" and during the Cheney - Bush era it was worth warm buckets of money.

To return to our premise about "thriving" another example is the nomination to the Governorship of Florida by the Republicans (who else)in August,2010.of one Rick Scott a previous owner and executive of the Columbia Healthcare Corporation that was fined ONE BILLION SIX HUNDRED MILLION DOLLARS for defrauding all American taxpayers through Medicare. Scott was not held ciminally responsible!

Scott stated during the court case maybe he should have watched his employees more carefully! Gee,do ya think? Of course in China he would have been executed, not treated to some 567,000 votes from the citizens of the state he helped defraud and serves now unappreciated by 65% of those who elected him.

Now- how idiotic can Americans be is a question yet to be answered. Another sickening question is why are the laws so constricted as to protect people like this from incarceration and personal responsibility and even more questionable is the personal values of voters who allow someone with this background into their lives, fortunes and futures with no qualms about how he will screw them again?

The fact is Mr. Scott spent millions of his fortune to get elected proving that money talks loudly in politics. And power can be more precious to some than money.

A fair question to the Pee Party novices elected in Nov. 2010 would be" where were your gonads and brains" when President of your party W. Bush and his oil mafia henchmen invaded Iraqnam promising that 60 to 80 billion dollars would be the total cost , also to be offset by profits from Oil derived from Iraq?(That did not happen,- other countries were awarded the major portions of drilling rights.)

Were TEA cortexes disconnected from your brains at that time, were you not Republicans? Did you not receive NRC mailing talking points keeping you abreast of these developments or didn't you even read newspapers or watch TV?

Did you talk amongst yourselves? Did you know about the cost of fighting the Afghanistan war for ten years or the cost of medicine and drug care for Seniors as passed by Republicans with no offsetting cuts or bargaining for drug costs? And the ongoing costs of that huge Bush tax cut for the wealthy?

Apparently the deaths of thousands of American troops , hundreds of thousands of innocent Iraq men women and children dying during this Trillion dollar fiasco and recon-struction costs did not impact your imagination enough to bring you to seek public office during that national elec-tion. Seemingly this was not offensive enough to your over-whelmingly Christian consciences?

Did it escape your attention that Comptroller of the US Treasury, David Walker appointed by your president Bush resigned in disgust in February of 2008 after warning in speeches advising the president, Congress and business groups for over a year that this nation was building toward a deficit exceeding 60 Trillion dollars making the 12 Trillion that you were so aghast at seem trivial when you were run-ning for Congress at rabble inspired Halloween like events supported by Fox news, childish signs picturing Obama as Hitler ,signs stating that Socialism was the current adminis-tration's design for America.

Do you know what socialism is? Are you aware socialist nations are far ahead of America in all categories of happi-ness and well being including retained monies?

You might ,being fair, now consider that the nations of the world leading in the"happiness index"(as well as wealth per capita) are socialist with the United States ranking 16th during the last year rated (2008,)New estimates would no doubt be far lower for America considering a ten percent unemployment rate and an increase in the US poverty level.

Returning to Comptroller David Walker he warned that each citizen's share of the US deficit was $175,000.including newborns.A family of four therefore owed in excess of $700,000 ,each American family has a net worth average of less than $90,000 meaning we have been bankrupt for years.

So will you please stop spreading the lie the Democrats and President Obama are responsible for our current condition?The past 30 months expenditures have been to prevent further deterioration of our auto industry and the banking system,these could have been lost to foreign investment without the money spent by the Democratic administration ,many states would have gone bankrupt - educational cuts and local services,teachers,and many other necessary services would have totally failed. Chaos could have ensued.

We are lucky to have survived as a nation. Ask Treasury Secretary Paulson!

A LOOK AT THE HEAD HOAXSTER
BEHIND THE LOBBYIST CURTAIN

"GROVEL NUTTWIST" Ne; Grover Norquist

I can feel it is safe to say this guy never had a lemonade stand on his front lawn or sold night crawlers for bait and never set up pins in a bowling alley after school .

His PLEDGE ISTHE HOAX since it PRETENDS that the signors will be supported by all neo con CONSERVATIVES forgetting that the same people put America in multiple losing wars and the largest deficit in American history and the greatest majority of voters despise this, CON OR NOT.

THIS IS INCLUDED IN MY BOOK SO YOU GET TO KNOW YOUR ENEMY ,the effete snob who tries to control Republicans through one issue to the detriment of Americans who vote.

This is not the controlling overreaching governance matter to most citizens .No Democrats respect or follow his dictates or principles . Look up a complete bio on the internet. His presence on the American political scene is nefarious and harmful in every way .

Grovel was the founder of a <u>taxpayer</u> <u>advocacy</u> group, <u>Americans for Tax Reform</u> in 1985. He was described by Associated Press reporter <u>Charles Babington</u> as "the driving force in pushing the <u>Republican Party</u> toward an ever-more rigid position of opposing any tax increase, of any kind, at any time."[

Background and Education

Norquist grew up in <u>Weston</u>, <u>Massachusetts</u>, the son of Carol (Lutz) and Warren Elliott Norquist. He attended <u>Weston High School</u>. His father served as vice president of <u>Polaroid Corporation</u>. He became involved with politics at an early age and in his early teenage years Norquist volunteered for the 1968 Nixon campaign, assisting with <u>get out the vote</u> efforts He enrolled at <u>Harvard University</u> in 1974, where he would obtain both a <u>BA</u> and <u>MBA</u>. While in school, Norquist was an editor at the *Harvard Crimson* and helped to publish the <u>libertarian</u>-leaning *Harvard Chronicle*. Norquist has said: "When I became 21, I decided that nobody learned anything about poli- tics after the age of 21.]* He attended the <u>Leadership Institute</u> in Arlington, Virginia,an organization that teaches conservative Americans how to influence public policy through activism and leadership.*Author's note;   In his case true,he did learn how to be a political huckster for money.

Americans for Tax Reform

Norquist is best known for founding Americans for Tax Reform in 1985, which he did at the request of President <u>Ronald Reagan</u>. The primary policy goal of Americans for Tax Reform is to reduce the percentage of the GDP consumed by the federal government. ATR states that it "opposes all tax increases as a matter of principle." Americans for Tax Reform seeks to curtail government spending by supporting <u>Taxpayer Bill of Rights</u> (TABOR) legislation and transparency initiatives and opposing cap-and-trade legislation and Democratic efforts to overhaul health care.

In 1993, Norquist launched his Wednesday Meetings series at ATR headquarters, initially to help fight President Clinton's healthcare plan and eventually becoming one of the most significant institutions in American conservative political organizing.

In 2009, Norquist received $200,000 in annual compensation for his part-time job (24 hours per week) with Americans for Tax Reform, plus an addition $22,419 other compensation from the organization and related organizations

Other Political Activities

Early in his career, Norquist was executive director of both the <u>National Taxpayers Union</u> and the national <u>College Republicans</u> organization, holding both positions until 1983. Afterward, he held the positions of Economist and Chief Speechwriter at the U.S. Chamber of Commerce from 1983 to 1984.[23]

Norquist traveled to several war zones across the world to help support anti-Soviet guerrilla armies in the second half of the 1980s. He worked with a support network for Col. Oliver North's efforts with the Nicaraguan Contras and other insurgencies, in addition to promoting U.S. support for groups including Mozambique's RENAMO and Jonas Savimbi's UNITA in Angola and helping to organize anti-Soviet forces in Laos.[12]

In addition to heading Americans for Tax Reform, Norquist serves on the board of numerous organizations, including the Hispanic Leadership Fund, Indian-American Republican Caucus, and The Nixon Center. He has long been active in building bridges between various ethnic and religious minorities and the free-market community through his involvement with organizations such as the Islamic Free Market Institute, ·Acton Institute, Christian Coalition and Toward Tradition. In business, Norquist was a co-founder of the Merritt Group, later renamed Janus-Merritt Strategies. [24]

Norquist also serves on the board of ParentalRights.org, a grassroots organization dedicated to adding a Parental Rights Amendment to the United States Constitution.

In 2010, Norquist joined the advisory board of GOProud, a political organization representing conservative gays, lesbians, transgendered people, and their allies, for which he was criticized by the Family Research Council.[25]

Norquist is a member of the board of directors of the National Rifle Association,[26] the American Conservative Union,[2] as well as the Advisory Council of GOProud,.[27]

Muslim Issues

Norquist is the co-founder of the Islamic Free Market Institute. [28]

In 2010, Norquist, whose wife was born into a Muslim family, emerged as the most outspoken Republican foe of politicizing the mosque-in-Manhattan issue, saying:

> "This is a distraction from a winning game plan... It is very stupid, when Republicans are poised to win an overwhelming victory in November over Democratic spending, to focus attention on this issue."[29]

He has also "announced his plan to assemble a center-right coalition to discuss pulling out of Afghanistan to save hundreds of billions of dollars."[30]

In a CPAC 2011 speech, David Horowitz accused Norquist of having connections with the Muslim Brotherhood.[31]

Influence in national politics

Working with eventual Speaker Newt Gingrich, Norquist was one of the co-authors of the 1994 Contract with America, and helped to rally grassroots efforts, which he later chronicled in his book *Rock the House*.[12] Norquist also served as a campaign staff member on the 1988, 1992 and 1996 Republican Platform Committees.[2]

Norquist was instrumental in securing early support for then Texas Governor George W. Bush, acting as his unofficial liaison to the conservative movement.[12] He campaigned for Bush in both 2000 and 2004.[32] After Bush's first election, Norquist was a key figure involved in crafting Bush's tax cuts. *The Wall Street Journal*'s John Fund dubbed him "the Grand Central Station" of conservatism and told *The Nation*: "It's not disputable" that Norquist was the key to the

Bush campaign's surprising level of support from movement conservatives in 2000.[33]

Norquist, along with Bill Kristol, Ralph E. Reed, Jr., Clint Bolick, and David McIntosh, is one of the so-called "Gang of Five" identified in Nina Easton's 2000 book by that name,[34] which gives a history of leaders of the modern, post-Goldwater conservative movement. Humorist P. J. O'Rourke has described Norquist as "Tom Paine crossed with Lee Atwater plus just a soupçon of Madame Defarge".[12]

Since Norquist's opposition to any and all tax increases implies that even deficit reduction agreements that are dominated by spending cuts should be rejected (since such agreements are still not entirely spending cuts), he has been identified by some policy makers as an obstacle to deficit reduction.[9][35]

Influence in state and local politics

Norquist's national strategy includes recruiting politicians at the state and local levels. Norquist has helped to set up regular meetings for conservatives in many states. These meetings are modeled after his Wednesday meetings in Washington, with the goal of creating a nationwide network of conservative activists that he can call upon to support conservative causes, such as tax cuts and deregulation. There are now meetings in 48 states.[36]

In 2004, Norquist helped California Governor Arnold Schwarzenegger with his plan to privatize the CalPERS system.[37] In Virginia's 2005 Republican primaries Norquist encouraged the defeat of a number of legislators who voted for higher taxes.[36]

Views on Government

Norquist favors dramatically reducing the size of the government.[12] He has been noted for his widely quoted quip: "I don't want to abolish government. I simply want to reduce it to the size where I can drag it into the bathroom and drown it in the bathtub."[38]

Some smaller government advocates argue that Norquist's "obsession with tax revenue" is actually counterproductive with respect to minimizing the size of government, however.[39] Although the Americans for Tax Reform mission statement is "The government's power to control one's life derives from its power to tax. We believe that power should be minimized."[40] Critics at the Cato Institute have argued that "holding the line on taxes constrains only one of the four tools (taxes, tax deductions, spending without taxation, and regulation) used by government to alter economic outcomes."[39]

Norquist published Leave Us Alone: Getting the Government's Hands Off Our Money, Our Guns, Our Lives,[41] in 2008. He has variously served as a monthly "Politics" columnist and contributing editor to The American Spectator.[42]

Involvement with Jack Abramoff

Norquist and Americans for Tax Reform were mentioned in Senate testimony relating to the lobbying scandal for which Abramoff pled guilty in 2006. Norquist has denied that he did anything wrong.[36] Records released by the Senate Indian Affairs Committee allege that ATR served as a "conduit" for funds that flowed from Abramoff's clients to surreptitiously finance grass-roots lobbying campaigns.[43]

Personal

On November 27, 2004, Norquist, then 48, married Samah Alrayyes[44]. Alrayyes is a Kuwaiti PR specialist who was formerly a director of the Islamic Free Market Institute and specialist at the Bureau of Legislative and Public Affairs at USAID. [45][46] Norquist is said to live a modest lifestyle. According to friend and former roommate John Fund, Norquist's devotion to conservative causes is "monk-like" and comparable to that of Ralph Nader.[12] Both of the Norquist children are adopted[47].

Norquist has competed three times in the comedy fundraiser "Washington's Funniest Celebrity" and placed second in 2009.[48][49] The Americans for Tax Reform Foundation also issued a $5,000 grant in 2009 to the Funniest Celebrity Charity Fund.[50]

AMERICAN SYSTEM OF JUSTICE ABOUNDS WITH LOVE AND PROTECTION FOR THE GUILTY

There are so many examples of how our justice system treats self evident criminals like children in kindergarten or virginal debutantes as they enter incarceration - the average American law abiding citizen should almost feel free to enter a life of crime ,especially if he has nothing to lose. At this point the writer,me ,is anticipating a rise in the crime rate an unintended consequence of the 8 years of Republican cruel rule.

In California many of the guilty depending on the severity of the crime are being set free by the thousands because there is no room in the prison system or funds to incarcerate.

The mental misfit Jared Loughner in Arizona is being treated for severe mental disorders in the hope to "cure" him enabling the prosecution to prevent a defense of insanity. The trial and defense will cost millions despite dozens of witnesses in broad daylight having witnessed the murders. This is depicted as a virtue by spokesmen of our Justice Department. Taxpayers know to the contrary.

The "underwear bomber"from Somalia who attempted to blow up an airliner with explosives lining his undergarment has not yet been put on trial and this is after two years in custody, His Father having ratted him out on the plot even before he boarded the plane and again numerous witnesses who were on the spot. He has decided to act as his own attorney despite being as dumb as a stump and surprisingly he has not yet asked to be given a Harvard Law school education in preparation.

Update Oct.,2011, the bomber has now decided to plead guilty and will be" given" life in prison Truly a gift.. flat TV screen and a gym work out daily? Watch and see.

We all could visit him on Saturdays and Sundays to see if he wants to convert to a religion that doesn't ask him to light up his gonads. After ten years he might see clear.

ARRIVAL OF A BLACK PRESIDENT
MEANS NEW WINGNUTS ARISING

America has an inborn racial problem in the south and in some Christian religions that have always felt the blacks ,negros ,niggers, spades, darkies, spooks, etc. are out to get the white man any way they can. "They will rob, rape and burglarize at any time and for any reason and cannot be trusted" but they are okay to dig ditches ,do gardening ,menial tasks and keep to themselves in their own ghettos and even serve in the military SO LONG AS THEY BEHAVE!

The impact of a mixed race black being elected president in America was beneficial and gratifying upon first view but in fact 54% of white males VOTED AGAINST Obama .And will again.

Black births are out polling white births so America will be majority non white in the next twenty five years. Then what happens to our poor bigots?

This partially explains why with Obama's election there has been an increase of crazies and groups of crazies and an increase in the purchase and carrying of firearms in vast areas of the nation that is unexplained since obviously just because there is a black president there is no foretelling an increase in crime. As a matter of fact major crimes in most areas including cities is down measurably in the past year and a half.

However the NRA has been pushing for all measures that increase the likelihood of gun sales for any reason and supporting those members of Congress who feel as they do because of NRA contributions to these gun whipped " public servants" in Congress.

The point is this – much of the redneck public in normal times is reactionary and ignorant ,not you ,Joe,the other guy! hence I employ the term crazies and the groups that have increased in numbers called "militias" increasing by about 80% in two years indicates that the NRA has done a job on the American public because that's who is joining these lethal groups.

In many states a felon out of prison can purchase a firearm legally. Makes him or her feel safe? Or is it a tool for work?

I ask anyone who thinks there is reason for militias what it is? What makes you think that a special band of locals with guns is needed where you live unless you are a cattle herder in some wild reaches of the far west or perhaps in the cattle spaces of Florida and you need to protect a herd or far flung farm or preserve.

Most militias are public because most of them are looking for as many members as they can persuade to join so they broadcast their existence and it gives them that macho air as a group. Many carry guns openly like 10 year old kids just to look strong and threatening. Go play guns. Bang,bang,you're dead.....

The fear that the government is going to seize their weapons is always and has been for decades one that is paramount, after all if you apply for a license of any sort the authorities will know who you are and where to grab your firearms so many "gunnies" shop at "gunshows"where no restrictions exist.

Does it ever occur to these folks that the government has tanks;, mortars, soldiers by the thousands.Their Hand guns ,rifles and piles of ammunition will be powerless against drones in the air armed with radar guided rockets which can render their groups useless in minutes if they assemble to show their ~``power"?

Senator Phil Gramm, CRACKER

John McCain, as presidential candidate named Phil Gramm as his closest economic counselor .In earlier years, a senator from Texas (there they are again)Gramm was the prime Republican force pushing through the Gramm-Leach-Bliley Act. It repealed the old Glass-Steagall Act, passed in the Great Depression, which prohibited a commercial bank from being in the investment and insurance business. President Bill Clinton cheerfully signed it into law, what was he thinking?

A year later Gramm as chairman of the Senate Banking Committee, attached a 262-page amendment to an omnibus appropriations bill, voted on by Congress right before a recess. The amendment received no scrutiny and duly became the Commodity Futures Modernization Act which okayed deregulation of investment banks, exempting most over the counter derivatives, credit derivatives, credit defaults, and swaps from regulatory scrutiny. Thus were born the scams that produced the debacle of Enron, a company on whose board sat Gramm's wife Wendy. She had served on the Commodity Futures Trading Commission from 1983 to 1993 and devised many of the rules coded into law by her husband in 2000. The Gramm crackers worked against true regulations,not for them. Bankers loved them.

Somewhat stained by the Enron debacle Gramm quit the senate in 2002 and began to enjoy the fruits of his own deregulatory efforts. He became a vice chairman of the giant Swiss bank UBS' new investment arm in the US, lobbying Congress, the Federal Reserve and the Treasury Department about banking and mortgage issues in 2005 and 2006, urging Congress to roll back strong state rules trying to crimp the predatory tactics of the subprime mortgage industry. UBS took a bath of about $20 billion in write offs from bad real estate loans this year.""

Gramm's the culprit in the lending/finance/GSE scam, though Clinton may be just as guilty since he approved the fiasco ,he had other things on his mind ? Idiotic.

DATA –TWSTED SISTERS IN TEXAS - OIL IS SLIPPERY slipping money to repubs

ON OIL COMPANIES ; THOUGHT YOU SHOULD KNOW American oil companies are totaling historic profits while Americans and the economy suffers.

Meanwhile, the oil industry is not using its profits to hire more people. RECENTLY Senator Paul falsely claimed the oil companies employ 9.2 million people — in fact, there are only 2.2 million jobs in the entire oil industry, and 40 percent of those jobs are minimum-wage work at gas stations. Exxon Mobil, Chevron, Shell, and BP have shed their U.S. workforce by 11,200 between 2005 to 2010, according to a report last year. Big Oil isn't investing in renewable energy or in reducing oil spills, either.And look who protects them and decries any effort to make them share the tax burden,"2 Guys from Texas"

while Kyl and Paul called an end to oil subsidies indefensible, they used the opportunity to label clean energy tax credits "crony government." During his rant against clean energy Paul said:

"It doesn't seem to be right that your tax dollars are sent to companies just because they're big contributors."

FACTS;

Republicans have received 88 percent of donations from the oil industry's coffers. In the Senate, Republicans have taken over $13.8 million from oil, compared to the Democrats' $3.3 million, meaning Senate Republicans have taken four times the amount in Big Oil contributions as Democrats. Kyl is the No. 29 largest recipient in the Senate from oil and gas in career contributions with over $330,000and Paul has received over $106,000 from oil. And tax credits are not"pay to" anyone with a name who is elected to Congress. Apples and oranges ,a politician's game.

DESTROY THE DEMOCRATS--

Seems like a Mafia method to me.

With the advent of a declared total warfare on the part of Republicans we find more and more headlines in the news about how President Obama can be finished off before he even starts his first year in office.

One Senator Dimwit(read Demented) states "the defeat of Healthcare overhaul will be Obama's Waterloo". Apparently defeating something that would be beneficial to the nation that would bring universal coverage for all as EVERY OTHER CIVILIZED NATION IN THE WORLD HAS IS THE AIM OF THE REPPUBLICAN PARTY AND THE HELL WITH THE SICK OR UNINSURED CITIZENRY.

There are dozens of other patterns of "DESTROY THE DEMOCRATS" cropping up in the media every day and it makes me wonder how the general population feels about such a stance on the part of a political group supposed to be devoting itself to the good of the overall populace of America .Their aim seems to be defeat anything supported by the Dems even if it is wonderful for the nation as long as it helps the R's get back into the Whitehouse and Congress

More examples-Let's destroy the appointments Obama makes to any court or any administration no matter what abilities or accomplishments-

Supreme Court nominee Sotomayor made a comment about Latina Women 8 years ago in a talk to a college, "this implies a bias that does not belong on the highest court in the land." Eight years for Chrisake?

And how does the Chief Justice of the Supreme Court feel about his wife heading up a radical group that would forbid abortions, do his personal feelings enter into the subject if it comes before the court? Think they talk on the pillow?

And how does he feel about corporations viz a viz the public good when it come up considering he represented them by the hundreds in previous appearances before federal courts?

And does cash for clunkers represent a boondoggle for buyers and dealers or a way of getting cars that burn gasoline up to 50% more than the new cars sold to the betterment of society as a whole and the nation or is it a "rip off" of the public money?

Republican Senators threatened a filibuster of the plan in the recent news headlines.

Perhaps this will bite them in the ass, I hope so. Their foresight is positioned in their anuses.

ANOTHER INCONVENIENT TRUTH FOR GOP NEOCONS

October 05, 2010 "Kabul Press" - -- The Pentagon will not tell the public what it costs to locate, target and kill a single Taliban soldier because the price-tag is so scandalously high that it makes the Taliban appear to be Super-Soldiers. As set out in this article, the estimated cost to kill each Taliban is as high as $100 million, with a conservative estimate being $50 million. A public discussion should be taking place in the United States regarding whether the Taliban have become too expensive an enemy to defeat.

Each month the Pentagon generates a ream of dubious statistics designed to create the illusion of progress in Afghanistan. In response this author decided to compile his own statistics. As the goal of any war is to kill the enemy, the idea was to calculate what it actually costs to kill just one of the enemy. The obstacles encountered in generating such a statistic are formidable. The problem is that the Pentagon continues to illegally classify all negative war news and embarrassing information. Regardless, some information has been collected from independent sources. Here is what we know in summary and round numbers:

1. Taliban Field Strength: 35,000 troops

2. Taliban Killed Per Year by Coalition forces: 2,000 (best available information)

3. Pentagon Direct Costs for Afghan War for 2010: $100 billion

4. Pentagon Indirect Costs for Afghan War for 2010: $100 billion

Using the fact that 2,000 Taliban are being killed each year and that the Pentagon spends $200 billion per year on the war in Afghanistan, one simply has to divide one number into the other. That calculation reveals that $100 million is being spent to kill each Taliban soldier. In order to be conservative, the author decided to double the number of Taliban being killed each year by U.S. and NATO forces (although the likelihood of such being true is unlikely). This reduces the cost to kill each Taliban to $50 million, which is the title of this article. The final number is outrageously high regardless of how one calculates it.

To put this information another way, using the conservative estimate of $50 million to kill each Taliban: Existing estimate of Taliban troops with no reinforcements 35,000 hard core in war zone.

It costs the American taxpayers $1 billion to kill 20 Taliban Extrapolating the figures   JUST KILLING EXISTING TALIBAN WOULD COST $1.75 TRILLION AND SEVENTEEN YEARS @2000 DEAD PER YEAR .THERE WOULD BE ADDED COST FOR AMERICAN DEAD BUT NO United States POLITICIAN WILL STAND FOR SUCH A DEBACLE. WE WILL LEAVE SOON! THERE IS NO PUBLIC SUPPORT FOR THIS WAR(look it up)

Lies,Liars,and the Association for THE BIG LIE thanks to Joseph Goebbels and now the Republican party.

The Nazi Party lives on in the hearts and minds of individuals like the George Bushes, Carl Rove and minions, paid for by manufacturers of war goods, drugs, medical equipment, certain banks and insurance companies supporting the R party.for the past half century or more.You can look it up.

The Nazi party knew if a lie was told often enough to listeners who were uneducated or willing to believe that which made them happy it would stick like superglue as the truth after a short period of time.

In a controlled nation there was no alternative to the lies put out by the Goebbels propaganda machine and effectiveness was nearly 100% during the Nazi reign.

However in America the Rove lying machine is not all powerful but it has it's strength In those who would like to believe it - many because it pays off in wealth of the realm or in the self deception of those who were raised to believe from birth .

During the health care debate in 2009 and on the Sarah Paleface lie about "Obama Death squads" was dumped like manure in the Midwest fields on the ill informed, especially senior citizens throughout the nation during the "Town Hall and Tea Party meetings",some supporters of reformed healthcare had ideas that older folks cannot get necessary medical care or operations even though they are needed because they are "too old".

To personally put the lie to this I had a hip replacement last year, two knees replaced and in the past month had six stents inserted due to a heart attack in Florida where I have no established doctor for heart care. I simply walked in off the street.. done in 24 hours,discharged in four days by one of the best specialists in the Central Florida area near Ocala and Orlando.There was no question about any of these operations as to necessity and absolutely no delay, paid by Medicare.

I am 78 years of age. And swimming four times a week at racing speed!

To; SUNDAY DIALOGUE-NYTIMES RE; WHICH WAY ON TAXES Nov.29,2011

AMERICAN RICH FOLKS are richer than ever

I must hasten to point out there is an outstanding and typical example of hypocritical self serving blather in the letter from the VP of Club for Growth printed on the date shown.

Those rule and regs and tax laws he decries have already been misshapen at his gang's behest, are already in place and have done nothing to cause the``rich" to start seeking new ways to evade taxes on their income since they have already paid lobbyists to promulgate mechanisms that make it easy as well as legal. Also it is a glaringly specious claim that the wealthy"create jobs ,a proven fallacy because the Bush tax cuts resulted in the fewest number of new jobs in any ten year period in a half century .Of course deficits soared, we saw jobs decrease .

Reagan tax` `reform" (300% increased deficit) that began class warfare a greedy 35 years ago and the Bush tax code rape of the muddled class in the past ten years has resulted in a lack of commercial activity by accumulating essential buying power in the hands of too few at the top 10% who already have what they want. Hence we have the closest scenario to a depression America has seen SINCE I WAS BORN IN 1932.

Purchasing power has gone to those who buy existing stocks and bonds, new industrial facilities are rare while internet schemes manipulating money in some form abound "full of sound and fury signifying nothing.", swaps and similar.

Reform the tax code? Laughable. Boehner wants to cut:"loopholes" and then lower the rates, MORE corporate profits , WORSE US deficits under the cloak of reform.

The most heinous example of a tax code gone insane is the one that permits one man to``earn" 5 Billion dollars and pay only a 15% tax on the amount in one year because he is involved in derivatives. .This astonishing example of ongoing greed exists because there were Republicans in charge of the crooked legalisms and lies necessary as groundwork to tax laws that make that crime "legal". There are countless disgusting examples throughout the annals of Wall Street's/ Congress's tax crime.

The Laffer curve of course has already been disproven as an outright appropriately named joke.

Smaller government?.This writer once had the opportunity to work briefly with the newly elected Governor of a Republican State who professed to that code. In eight years State employees went from about 6,000 to over 12,000. Whoops! (to quote our Texas governor)

Finally, Growth Club, how about a return to the tax code of the era before Reagan, we had won a massive war and were rebuilding Europe (Marshall plan), ,.the US Highway system and new industry was springing up, returning GIs went to college free with jobs plentiful. And the wealthy were "rich" just the same. And most folks had decent incomes .And jobs.

JACK DOYLE

Other Republican fairy tales include President Reagan's intelligence on tax and business matters.Take a look at the chart in this book about unemployment ,GDP ,etc .from the Congressional record.

One GOP devotee I know personally thought "Bush seems sincere" so he voted for him. After the 8 horrible years following he said to me quietly that he could not see any way out of the deficit situation , I did not call him out for the mess he helped create (TWICE).He is a millionaire through inheritance and investments. His son in law who during the same conversation in passing commented on money appropriated for the Education department budget that it would be"frittered away"(an amount in the billions) and Reagan "knew how to create jobs from the bottom up"- ,gag me with a short handled shovel .

As is Republican habit it seems he forgot the Reagan depression when unemployment was over ten percent and mortgages were 20% thanks to Reagan appointed Federal reserve chairman Paul Volcker who dragged on the calamity for almost three years thereby adding trillions to the US deficit. I do not believe that putting a large percentage of working Americans out of useful employment and paying them enough to live on for a year or more while creating a recession by increasing the cost of money and the profit gained by loaning it can do anything but depress the efficiency of an economy and the standard of living for citizens of the nation .Analysis of what occurred in our country after Volcker and Greenspan forced higher interest rates on business and citizens convince me I am correct. Both Fed heads ultimately had to cut rates drastically to get the country functioning again though at lower standards which is a consequence of deliberate recessions.

The Reagan Years

	1977–80	1981–83	CHANGE
Real GNP	+3.2%	+1.3%	-59%
Industrial Production	+3.0%	+0.1%	-97%
Rate of Capacity Utilization	83.4%	75.9%	- 9%
Plant & Equipment Expenditures	+14.6%	.8%	-95%
Housing Starts	1.76mil	1.28mil	-27%
Domestic Auto Sales	8.48mil	6.25mil	-26%
Business failures	8461	24491	+189%
Civilian unemployment	6.5%	9.0%	+ 38%
Number of persons unemployed	6.74mil	9.89mil	+ 47%
Real disposable income	+1.9%	+1.3%	- 32%
Prime Rate	10.96%	14.84%	+35%
Federal Budget deficit	$48.5bil	$153.0bil	+215%
Farm Income	+1.75%	-5.7%	-326%

(Source: Congressional Record, 3/26/84. Each figure is an overall or annual average in order to offset any difference which would arise due to the variance in the number of years of each administration.

The shooting of an elected American House of Representative member by a GUN DEVOTED deranged 22 year old man has proven the horrible truth that there is no safety in this nation. Not for duly elected representatives of tens of thousands of people , not for Presidentially appointed judicial officials or innocent 9 year old schoolchildren all of whom happen to be in a public place on a Saturday morning, exercising their right of free assembly.

Sadly and Ironically Congresswoman Gabrielle Giffords was presumably "privileged " to read out the second amendment portion of the American Constitution in Congress a few days before her near assassination in Tucson, Arizona ,

Arizona is a beautiful but sorry State that has no carry laws for firearms . Arizona seethes with hate for any number of reasons including the well known fact it is full of illegal aliens from Mexico who have inundated the area for decades and the population suffers from a high unemployment rate over ten percent but guns are as accessible (to the ill educated and even the undetected possibly drug addicted) as chewing gum or a pair of hedge clippers.

Representative Giffords, targeted for death by a poster goblin of insanity has publicly proclaimed PROUD ownership and ability to use a Glock automatic,ironically the type of gun she was mortally wounded with. The population wide ownership of guns of all description makes all citizens of Arizona an open target anytime and anyplace, restaurants, businesses ,taverns or church. That includes those who own and carry a weapon or leave it at home for nighttime protection only.

The patriotic rabble babble about our soldiers overseas making us safe or safer is so much profit gaining propaganda by those corporate sponsored politicians PAC groups that would perpetuate our presence in over 400 overseas military installations throughout the world for their own profitable multifarious purposes. And FOREVER!. All while state,local and national laws permit easily concealed inexpensive weapons of mass murder available to just about anyone without permits or registration in many cases. All because Presidents who have been shot by the insane (Reagan) and Congresspersons who have lost part of their brains to bullets(Tucson AZ Representative Giffords) favor the right to bear arms ! Insanity and illogic reigns.

Guns are universally available now and are legal only recently because of the grotesque misinterpretation of the Constitution of the United States concerning the outdated useless armed "militias "by a small group of Republican appointed"Supreme Court justices "who apparently are in love with corporations including the one feared by most legislators of any party, the National Rifle Association whose sole avowed purpose is to render any law restricting guns of any kind impossible at any level. NRA purposes are not for hunting guns but for selling weapons that kill.

The current interpretation of the 2nd Amendment pretends that almost any citizen has the right to bear arms even in the absence of any militia, such Colonial or Confederate armed groups having fallen into disfavor or nonexistence over 100 years ago.

EACH ELECTED REPRESENTATIVE of the people of the United States of America has a duty to protect citizens and themselves against the mounting death toll of this maniacal liberalization of the freedom to bear arms.We are in danger of losing freedom from fear and civilization as we know it. Polls show the public would overwhelmingly welcome moves against the NRA and the terrible LIBERALS who have forced and finagled this madness on America, the previously Beautiful.

The Honorable Gabrielle Giffords

U.S. House of Representatives

1030 Longworth House Office Building

Washington, DC 20515

Jan. 24, 2012

Dear Gabby

Most Americans regret you are leaving Congress but I and millions of others understand considering the irrationality of the organization since the advent of the Teaparty elected by Fox News in the lower house government. Your life and full recovery are certainly paramount.

At this critical time in our history the question arises who better than you to assist in the effort that must be made against many of the onerous gun "freedoms" that have resulted in maniacs like Jared Laughner walking undetected amongst the citizenry with a weapon that can dispense enough kill power to wipe out a platoon in less than a minute with no prohibition against carrying same into any area.

As these "freedoms" continue thousands more innocent unsuspecting Americans will die for NRA profits and for that monetized reason alone. Meanwhile many peaceful persons in Arizona and elsewhere are now already afraid to walk the streets under the martial law combat conditions. Should middle aged, ,60 and 70 year old citizens be forced to arm themselves out of fear, spending hundreds or thousands of dollars they do not have for fear of the unknown, further endangering themselves and others?

Congresswoman Carolyn McCarthy, Mayor of NYC Bloomberg and his group,, the National Police Chiefs Assn. and many other groups will welcome your support and you have pain based facts first hand on your side that make sense in the battle against loaded gun " open carry " anarchy in the streets. It is obvious even if you had your own Glock loaded under the table at the public meeting you may not have had a chance to defend yourself. Therefore owning and carrying a gun renders even armed citizens to attack to similarly weaponized menacing evil intending individuals.

Guns spread all over the land due solely to the deliberate misreading of the Constitution encouraging weaponry in the hands of "militias" that are no longer needed or in existence are killing, ruining the lives and endangering the people who you were sworn to protect.,as are legal armor piercing bullets.INSANE!

The current so called "SUPREME" court has it's own corporate inspired agenda and not one promoting the formation of a perfect union ,liberty, justice ,harmony or tranquility. This should be obvious to all except those who gain by it. Americans urgently need you to join in an effort to disarm those who would do us harm by UNCONTROLLED gunfire for profit ! Meaningful change in this weapon culture will take years, courage and strong people like yourself but it must start now, it is already overdue because of greed and the profit motive.

Sincerely,

Jack Doyle

TRULY SORRY TO BE HERE –Think about Scandanavian countries.

From the standpoint of a human being unfortunately a citizen of the United State of America this writer is disgusted with the majority of Americans most (on a percentage basis) of whom are against government sponsored healthcare calling it derisively " Obamacare" as if the half black president made it up on his own with no assistance from thousands of knowledgeable people from appropriate backgrounds in both parties .By the way including Mitt Romney ,former governor of Mass., the installer of a similar plan in that state which has worked well since 2006 benefitting Republicans and Democrats at reasonable cost.

Many Americans use the term OBAMACARE as a derogatory term because of the color of Obama's skin. That secretly explains why they are against anything he sponsors even if it has been proposed by white Republicans in previous years as in this case(Nixon, Reagan. Bush and others proposed similar plans)) You can look it up! Meanwhile America will be minority white in 25 years like South Africa .

What is more disturbing most critics ARE IGNORANT of what the plan entails and have never looked at it on the government website or on AARP where it appears in condensed but accurate form. And most of it is not yet law.? What is wrong with this picture?-They're afraid it might be a good plan they like.

You must remember the plan of the vanquished GOP survivors from the last presidential election to oppose everything Democratic in all venues being a scorched earth plan of Carl Rove mounting a negative public relations advertising attack on broad fronts sponsored by corporate supporters of the Republican party.The bullpen of future Republican presidential hopefuls (Palen,Huckster,etc.) on Fox News,TV,Internet radio and newspaper mounted every lie or half truth attacking government sponsored healthcare as if were a secret plan to infect every citizen with a fatal disease.

And at this moment National Healthcare Insurance is challenged by 26 Republican States (with fifty million of their citizens with no coverage at all) and on the Republican biased supreme Court Docket for final closing arguments by July1,2012 .Meanwhile all the world's free countries have enjoyed just such a plan for 20,30,40 years and wonder at the United States displaying such ignorance having lost thousands of lives and trillions of dollars for the lack of it.

Obviously DEAD CITIZENS DO NOT DISIMAY REPUBLICANS.!

A U.S. nuclear weapons assembly plant in California is off limits to any kind of photography, information gathering, or reporting. Local residents are unaware of the plant's existence and its potential radiological hazards. (Repost from Indymedia NL)

Current production is of a yield of thirty Hiroshima equal explosions in one compact delivery mechanism.

Lockheed/Martin are the makers of these useless and unused fearsome bombs.POTLACH,not really,no other nation has as many Atomic warheads as does the United States of Futility. It's good to know we have kept up production and will not run out as the current administration is dismantling them hundreds at a time along with Russia.

WHEN WE VOTED FOR A REPUBLICAN AND SUPPORTED HIM WITH SIZEABLE CHECKS

Back in the day when George W.Bush was running against John McCain in the GOP primary, year 2000 my wife and

I both sent what for us were large amounts of money to the McCain primary campaign. We both had seen the so called accomplishments of Junior as Governor of Texas knowing W's gaining the position ,his previous occupations in the oil industry and baseball was due to his Father's friends and their joined money and of course influence from daddy's election as Congressman and then VP to President Reagan, budget buster.

W's term as an oil industry VP resulted in the company going bankrupt .His presidency of the Texas Rangers Baseball team when he left to run for governor reveals the firm had never had a profit, the team was millions of dollars in deficit and decades later it still is. Sound familiar?

Back to our voting, we were appalled at the treatment Carl Rove gave to McCain when it came to the important South Carolina primary where it has been famously broadcast that McCain was accused of being mentally ill, that he had fathered a black illegitimate child (McCain and his wife had adopted a Bangladesh child) and his wife Cindy was a drug addict. McCain lost South Carolina. There were other nefarious tactics employed.This can be reviewed in detail on the internet-Wilkopedia.

Rotten Rove inspired maliciously evil deeds in that still Confederate state killed McCain's candidacy in a hurry. In two months John dropped his campaign , became a reluctant tepid Bush supporter as his Father In Law was a died in the wool R supporter financially for decades and McCain had to be a team player.

When McCain's Headquarters called me later for support financially for his incumbent run as Senator I told them I knew how and why he had lost in the primary and couldn't understand how he would associate himself with the Republican party after the character assassination they subjected him to. I suggested he change his party which idea went nowhere though I brought it up in a second phone call.

Four years later politically Bush seeking his second term told McCain that brother Jeb Bush was not going to run for president (he had two children with publicly known newspaper reported drug problems,wonder why?) and the establishment Bush group would support him in 2008 which "turned "McCain into an avid supporter of the Iraqnam war after his initial continuing rejection of that fiasco. Flip flopping is inbred in Republican office seekers.

So would it surprise you to learn we learned to despise the Republicans.? My question is why did nearly half the voters go for a useless reformed drunk fratboy .? Did they have any idea about his lack of success in previous endeavours? Does anyone read out there or is America trapped in Foxedup news network?

Had it not been for the "tie" with Gore and a daddy Bush appointed Supreme court "Justice" kicking the election to junior out of loyalty we would have had President Al Gore who never would have thought about invading Iraq. Nor would John McCain if he had won the nomination and the Presidency for the GOP. So we see it pays to be connected and it would pay America to pass a law prohibiting immediate relatives of former Presidents running for the office. The rulership of royalty has stained and ruined every country that ever was governed by it as has imitation royalty. We have suffered enough already, please no more!

Lesser offices have also suffered from inept and corrupt management because of nepotism practiced in selections of relatives for State offices,Congressmen and Senators during loose primary methods in the "wilds" of some of our diverse areas of America.

POLITICIAN(Webster definition) a person primarily interested in political office for SELFISH OR OTHER NARROW SHORT SIGHTED REASONS.

pp⤶Wilkopedia statistics POLITICIAN Other def) War whore Cheney spouts lies "THAT WHICH MAKES ONE FEEL GOOD "--- AMERICAN IDIOTS

The costs of the War on Terror are often contested, as academics and critics of the component wars (includ- ing the Iraq War) have unearthed many hidden costs not represented in official estimates. The most recent major report on these costs come from Brown University in the form of the Costs of War project,[1] which said the total for wars in Iraq, Afghanistan, and Pakistan is at least $3.2-4 trillion.[2] The report disavowed previous estimates of the Iraq War's cost as being under $1 trillion, saying the Department of Defense's direct spending on Iraq totaled at least $757.8 billion, but also highlighting the comple- mentary costs at home, such as interest paid on the funds borrowed to finance the wars and a potential nearly $1 trillion in extra spending to care for veterans returning from combat through 2050.[3]

Those figures are significantly more than typical estimates published just prior to the start of the Iraq War, many of which were based on a shorter term of involvement. For example, in a March 16, 2003 Meet the Press interview of Vice President Dick Cheney, held less than a week before the Iraq War began, host Tim Russert reported that "every analysis said this war itself would cost about $80 billion, recovery of Baghdad, perhaps of Iraq, about $10 billion per year. We should expect as American citizens that this would cost at least $100 billion for a two-year involvement.".

US = US SUCKERS.

A RECENT PUBLICATION ON GLOBALIZATION

The book written by an " expert "on world affairs and the bush administration of 2002-2009 treats with flat earth theories and counterinsurgency efforts that are ongoing and proposed for future consideration. The tome mentions a "BIBLE " on counterinsurgency and intimates progress has been made against BinLaden's Al Qaeda.

The 'BIBLE' was published in 1964 so judging by what is happening in Iraq, Afghanistan , Pakistan and other hellholes as this is written no one in command seems to be taking the bible into consideration as we battle suicidal terrorists on their own turf and at hours of their choosing as we fight a holding or losing battle on every front It seems to be outdated or non applicable before our military is aware of it.

Our military has been decimated and demoralized for at least 4 years now with 2,3 and 4 tours of duty overseas in fighting zones with suicides and divorce rates in military families soaring with no end in sight.

So we continue to build a fighting machine over supplied with armaments from the second world war and duplications of aircraft even the Pentagon does not want. Wonder why we are broke?

The best counterinsurgency (COIN) efforts so far are bribing the backward religiously insane tribes and clans to cease fire in Iraq (the Baath bunch) and to join the Shiite government that seems engorged with stupidity and corruption. Some of it is inspired by our tax dollars spread thin in the muddle east and there is never enough.

This is another block in the building of our Dungeon of Debt that we never could afford and certainly cannot now.

A concurrent unaffordable structure is our half billion dollar embassy that will take thousands of personnel to staff for the next half century .Many American diplomats have refused to serve in any of the Arab countries and this is just part of the ongoing problem. And it never seems to occur to our nation and it's leader that as we maintain a force of some 300,000 troops and mercenaries at cost of $ a million each per year (plus dead, wounded and dismembered) that Iraq has some 26 million souls many of whom fought a battle against Iran for seven years with more than 700,000 casualties led by none other than Saddam Hussein.

The Iraqi army had no training by US forces. The government had and has no constitution, no democracy or elections but they continued to fight because they had to .With soldiers as young as ten or eleven.

And at present our military says the Iraqis are not yet ready to protect themselves after years of American military "assistance and training"? Can we get out,yes and accept the consequences before they are worse.

The answer is we must get out a la Nixon/Vietnam with a promise of atomic retribution if the area becomes a haven for leaders of terror. A middle east Marshall plan could be the carrot before the stick as we wean ourselves off foreign oil and the wealth of the oil barons dissipates. This will add to our debt but can pay off in the next century.

What if our payments for oil were trimmed by 30% or more and we established a lend lease reconstruction program along with grains and foods from our overstocked farms and silos equal to that reduction.

At the same time our insane building up to a trillion dollars in defense spending would diminish. Sound impossible? How would you have imagined the place we are in now in 1999 when all we had to concern ourselves with was the trumped up concern about the coming year 2000 in our computer oriented society?

A gallon of gasoline was a buck at the tank and heating oil was cheap along with natural gas? And unemployment was non existent and home prices were stable?

And the US Treasury actually paid off part of our National Debt during the Clinton administration as comments were being made by fiscal geniuses like Alan Greenspan and Paul Voelker that we should not pay off the national debt too quickly because it might cause a worldwide panic? Oh, the good old days!

As we go to publication the projected hypothetical (imaginery) budget for our wars and the Pentagon has been constricted by half a trillion dollars over ten years by Congressional action andlo and behold Republicans who agreed to it less than 12 months ago are fighting to change their so called minds. The some 92 Peeparty delegates wanted drastic reduction of the US deficit and forced the hand of both parties during a last minute sword of Damocles debate fiasco that President Obama should have terminated by executive fiat considering the low intellect of the minority 92 Peepartiers.

The debt ceiling itself is unconstitutional. Having the White House declare the debt limit unconstitutional is "going to get a pretty strong second look as a way of saying, 'Is there some way to save us from ourselves?'" -Sen. Chris Coons (D-Del.). The constitutional argument stems from a phrase in the 14th Amendment: "The validity of the public debt of the United States, authorized by law, including debts incurred for payment of pensions and bounties for services in suppressing insurrection or rebellion, shall not be questioned."Obama could have stopped the debate by the Fourteenth amendment action but had no stomach or backing for it.

In the future this may become a stonewall Presidential argument along with a halt to the illegal filibuster anachronism that has held American progress hostage for 36 long months .

America desperately needs such an action. A majority should be what is needed to transact normal business of state.Treating bills in the House and Senate as if they were declarations of war or Amendments to the Constitution is legislative stone age practice of the Republicans wrongly agreed to by the president and his party. It has cost Americans so very dearly the tally cannot be measured.

AN AMERICAN EXPATRIATE STATEMENT; "AMERICA'S A NICE PLACE TO VISIT BUT"

I wouldn't want to live there.

The two countries that the United States destroyed in WW2 nearly seven decades ago enjoy another five years life expectancy and spend almost 30% less on medical expenses, their deaths at child birth are over 50% lower than in America the beautiful. They have had free publicly paid medical care for over 50 years. Germany had it in Bismark's time.That was 1840.

Germany and Japan where young citizens are far less likely to be involved in military operations that create death and permanent disabilities used to be more martial but they learned from their mistakes. By treaty in defeat they gave up on military buildups forever!

Japanese , Germans and other nationalities are far less obese than Americans hence enjoy longer lives. On a happiness scale they are in the top whereas Americans are ranked at 16 from the top and going further down the scale due to unemployment and poverty due to endless wars and disastrous political tax management in our country.

Most other nations are also not caught up in political actions by ill informed citizenry like the Peeparty against the very tax system that keeps their government functioning.

They have not been persuaded to prevent improvements to a poorly functioning expensive health care system by bringing lawsuits by deliberately invective elected leaders who oppose the improvements in the hopeof future election victories.

PLEASE, Facefacts, Republican Romneycare is "Obamacare", it is appreciated by over 90% of the people who enjoy it in Mass . AND IT WORKS TO THE BENEFIT OF ALL. This in spite of protestations to the contrary.

To Continue:

in other countries firearms are not encouraged publicly in demonstrations or coffee houses and cannot be purchased like cigarettes or chewing gum by demonstrably insane or mentally ill citizens or those who have a background of crime. Guns can be purchased by Federally listed terrorists ,believe it or not.

And other national borders are not wide open to over half a million illegal entrants each year who infiltrate their job market at lowest wages, emergency free medical care and education for their illegal offspring who do not speak "American" or English.

Making matters worse, American local governments must provide special programs to these people who are actually invading them with little impediment by local law or ineffective federal border protection.. And of course taxes paid by US citizens pay for many benefits to illegals.

In the past ten years there have been some steps taken to halt the onslaught of illegals but the problem still exists for pre existing political/commercial reasons still unresolved. No country with thousands of miles of wilderness borders can prevent immigration by itself especially when there is a nucleus of millions already ensconced in the American business system integral to portions of the unwilling host nation ,some or many of them with dual citizenry and roots in America.

The granting of automatic citizenship to those born here of illegal parents is a Gordian knot, it has led to a nearly impossible situation for the American people from a legal and moral standpoint. Furthermore the estimate of twelve million illegal immigrants here is possibly more than fifty percent underestimated.

CHAPTER 5

Feb2012

Messy Republicans

As bad as the Slate of Republican candidates for president have proven(remember how taken primary voters were with the governor of Texas until"whoops''and other episodes and Pizzaman Caine,the flirty flirty guy with the flirty flirty pie?And how impossible 999 was when a calculator was used? Republicans can't seem to keep from peeing in the soup.

Take a look at Governor Corpulent Christy's plans for the NJ Budget -2012. Tax cuts up to ten percent mostly larger for the richest in the state and all while the state has a longtime deficit in pension obligations equaling 150% of the entire state budget for the year and also while the Transportation fund is flat broke and in need of millions .And there are a few billion bucks missing to balance the"balanced"(according to his advertising on TV) budget. Today New Jersey's most uncouth chief exec said "Warren Buffett should write a check and shutup!"qualifying him as an expert in budgeting. In case you haven't noticed he is a serial large mouthed liar as opposed to large mouthed bass tard.

In another unfortunate GOP state Hailey Barbour has released numerous convicted killers by pardon as he departs his position as Governor of Mississippi causing an appeal to The State Supreme Court for substantial reasons by the only Democrat on the State executive payroll,the Attorney General of the poverty stricken state. Hearings are now open and victims of the parolees and their families await results,. To the dismay of the victims and their families the court has ruled they have no jurisdiction? Ex governor Barbour is typical of Republican politicians in the worst way possible.

Another sad case-the least educated State in the US in my opinion,having lived there where employees of shoe stores did not know what a shoehorn was.,S.C governor Nikki Haley struggles to keep ahead of bad polls(in a state where

A " cadaver" was elected to the US Senate for 54 years running-dying in office at age 102)This was Strom Thurmond, Mr. Tobacco.

By WAYNE WASHINGTON - wwashington@thestate.com

CURRENT POLITICAL FACTS ABOUT SOUTH CAROLINA;

Poll: More disapprove of Haley's job performance than approve . SURPRISE?

By WAYNE WASHINGTON - wwashington@thestate.com South Carolinians have soured on Nikki Haley, turning the relatively new governor from a national Tea Party favorite into a chief executive struggling to maintain support among members of her own party, the latest Winthrop University poll shows.

Only 34.6 percent of those surveyed — 1,073 registered S.C. Democrats, Republicans and independents — said they approved of Haley's job performance, according to the poll. Far more — 43 percent — said they disapprove of the way the Republican is handling her job as governor. The poll's margin of error was plus or minus 2.9 percent percentage points.

Haley's approval rating is lower than that of President Barack Obama, a Democrat in a longtime GOP state.

So on to the deeper south where the gubernatorial unhappiness is stronger.

Florida Gov. Scott has not endorsed an R presidential candidate and has scarcely acknowledged the feverish pitch that is now enveloping the race.

Political analysts state he is doing this for practical reasons,: Mr. Scott, 59, remains a sorry polarizing figure in Florida, and his approval ratings float around the 30 percent mark,of no benefit for any of the four candidates.

May I call attention to Florida's Governor Scott's HCA Columbia Healthcare firm -fined one billion,eight hundred million dollars for Medicare fraud qualifying him in the state most deeply dependent on Medicare disbursement for the job of governor, possible the hot FLA sun maybe affected the voters. The judge and jury in the fraud case also must have frazzled- could have been sun stroke or ?

Gov. Scott has not endorsed a R presidential candidate and has scarcely acknowledged the feverish pitch that is now enveloping the race.

Just one set back for this governot is citizen response to his medicare plans in the state. 71 Percent of Florida Voters Oppose Medicaid Reimbursement Cuts to Hospitals,a New Poll Shows.

They fear loss of specialized healthcare services that benefit all, view Medicaid favorably

TALLAHASSEE, Fla., Feb. 6, 2012 /PRNewswire/ -- Seventy-one percent of Florida voters say Medicaid is an important program that should be maintained and oppose the deep reimbursement cuts to Florida's hospitals that Governor Rick Scott and legislative leaders are proposing this session, a new poll shows.

Voters say they are most concerned that additional reimbursement cuts will force hospitals to eliminate specialized healthcare services such as trauma care, advanced care for newborn babies, burn units and outpatient clinics.

The poll also found that 72 percent of voters oppose Governor Scott's proposal to reduce the number of days that Medicaid patients can behospitalized annually from 45 to 23 days. After 23 days, hospitals would no longer receive Medicaid reimbursement for these patients. Over 75% of Florida Voters Oppose Medicaid Reimbursement Cuts to Hospitals,a New Poll Shows.

And the parade continues,

We have another state afflicted with Republican governor regret ,the Great Lakes area where people did something, namely

1 million signatures collected for Wisconsin governor recall

(January 17, 2012 | From Paul Steinhauser, CNN)

More than a million people have signed a petition to recall Wisconsin's governor, the state's Democratic Party said Tuesday.

That's nearly twice the 540,208 signatures required to seek a recall of first-term Republican Gov. Scott Walker, who drew the ire of labor unions and public school teachers after he stripped public employees of their collective bargaining rights.

State Democratic Party officials said they would submit the signatures by close of business Tuesday. The officials also said they would turn in more than the required number of signatures needed for recall elections for the state's Republican lieutenant governor and three state senators.

And governor Scott Walker of Wisconsin has failed after trying to delay his recall ,one million signatures for same have been received by the state,nearly twice the number required for the motion. Much cash from corporate front PACS has flowed to this lackey to support his union breaking efforts.It appears a dead heat in June of 2012.

5 DUMBOCRACY NOT AS ENVISIONED

Another glaring lack in the Democratic system is the lack of incentive for citizens to cast votes diluting the good and promoting the bad in governance.

More than a dozen states have passed laws in Republican legislatures through various subterfuges like requiring a photographic " votercard" or a birth certificate by those casting a vote.These new "voter fraud" laws seek to disenfranchise the poor and elderly,college students and the young who have difficulty in accessing such documents.

The pretext of voter fraud is fraud itself as there is no evidence of

more than a few illegally cast votes in any elections in all covered voting districts over the past decade.This concerted effort is directed by Carl Rove to prevent Democratic votes now and in the future. The Federal election commission now is seeking to overturn these transparent efforts to control elections.

Some nations have a penalty for not voting and get a participation rate in the 90

percentile range, In a less demanding America we should give an incentive of tax credits for voting in National and state elections increasing them after for instance 5 continuous votes, then ten, etc. Such a plan would encourage more interest in candidates' views and keep voters up on the promises made and kept in selected election campaigns as time goes on.

Participative Democracy is badly needed here as witness where the majority of citizens until late 2008 thought that Saddam Hussein had responsibility for the Twin Towers destruction, also that we had found weapons of mass destruction in Iraq. FOX?

Such ignorance is unconscionable except for the fact that the Republican administration propaganda machine deliberately kept these myths alive for as long a they could including outright lying whenever possible.

While I'm at it with reference to faults in American democracy the Jury system is another problem that needs attention that no one in authority is willing to give it.

Adversary proceedings with winner take all thrust (guilty or not guilty) encourage prosecutors to withhold evidence, coach witnesses to lie and simply adopt a winner take all attitude and the same holds true for poorly paid defense councils who are many times appointed by law to the "indigent."

Cuts in budgets on all levels threaten capable legal reps for those who cannot afford one.

Juries do not have the technical knowledge they need to settle and adjudicate complicated scientific and medical cases and must rely on evidence without referring to further study or testimony of unbiased scientists,doctors ,specialists etc. who have no self interested point to make.They are in all cases paid by one side or the other and dueling experts confuse jurors.

Juries cannot question witnesses or dueling attorneys.

The Menendez Brothers and O.J. Simpson trials in California were a perfect example of the twisting of justice because juries were subpar in performance intellectually.

Many Countries have trial by a jury of pro jurists, judges who know the law and can ask questions at appropriate times which jurors can not .All courtroom actors are seeking justice and the truth and represent the public interest though the defense will take the side that makes the defendant look innocent as much as possible.

Another poorly thought out facet of our justice system is the election of judges based on advertising and campaigns by the candidates who in many county (parish) or townships are not required to have any legal education whatsoever .They can be tailors, mechanics or farmers and as long as they say the pleasing(politic) thing in their campaigns and get enough votes-----------

"HERE COME THE JUDGE."

A recent case that was a miscarriage of justice had to be brought to the Supreme Court to make it right. Even there the case was close, the decision was split 5 to 4 involving a case in the West Virginia supreme court Chief Justice Brennan presiding. Brennan after having benefited from THREE MILLION DOLLARS spent on advertising advocating his reelection by the defendant Massey Coal. in Brennan did not recuse himself from a decision that threw out a FIFTY MILLION DOLLAR award to be paid by Massey to the plain-tiff coal companies who were harmed by fraud by the big spending Massey defendant.

Sadly most Americans are unaware that KING COAL, ASTHMA INDUCER IS SEEKING TO RULE THE LAND led by the ever prominent greedy Koch Brothers,multibillion dollar corporation.

The sophistry of the claim that the first amendment sup-porting free speech as it has newly been interpreted by the corporately controlled United States Supreme Court enables advertising for candidates for any office and in this case a judge as long as that service is not paid by the candidate. This masquerade makes free speech an expansive WEALTH DRIVEN right of the wealthiest as opposed to a small group of 2 or 200 people who can only afford a dollar per person while another can spend millions through "focus groups" or facades of any kind. They "focus" all right. Spelled with --ck .

HEADLINE RE TERRORISM

London still aghast examining American logic for Iraq war and search for weapons of MASS DECEPTION

In spite of Tony Boy's (Blair's) love of bushman's war and support for it with English war deaths (I smell the blood of many Englishmen and some millions of pounds lost as well) there is at this writing an exhaustive 9 month hearing concerning the entire bloody mess being conducted in London, an "official inquiry"into the war.The lack of reasoning and twisted thinking,lack of logic for this war that helped tear down the American economy and cost thousands of lives of US Troops and hundreds of thousands of Iraqi soldiers and civilians was last week pointed out by one superintellect named Hans Blix, the Swedish diplomat who led the UN body that scoured the Iraq countryside far and wide for what proved to be figments of bush's imagination and of his ass kissing advisors .Even Colin Powell was duped into believing a milk truck contained war making chemicals proudly pointed out same to the world during a famous TV presentation,as I recall at the UN. Such worldwide embarrassment.

During testimony Blix called the arguments for war absurd and described Britain as a prisoner on the American train. His disdain for both top heads of state was blatantly not hidden

Wonder how the Brits got hoodwinked into this? Now as a hypothesis imagine if the bushman took Tony Boy aside and gave him some inside stock tips on what his daddy's Mutual fund was buying into on the strength of advance knowledge concerning war plans, could that not help induce English participation in this useless war that has yet to end? Especially if the tip made clear VP Cheney,the Crown Princes of Saudi Arabia, Wolfie Wolfowicz of the World Bank ,Rumdum Rumsfeld and several other important folks were in the same money grabbing scheme? Is this farfetched or good reasoning? And how would anyone ever ever know? Did the "lapdog" get more than his bone?

The inquiry of course is a striking case of locking the barn door after the entire barnful of animals are stolen and the barn burned to the ground.

COMING SOON IN A FAILING GOVERNMENT TOO NEAR YOU !

"Noogie" (My nickname) Nuttwist Norquist, the anti tax demon has struck again entering the United(?) States Congress's argument about the 2012 never to be passed budget. This pudgy effete snob pimping for Americans For Tax Reform is a perfect example of what comes from the spoiled wealthy upbringing of a person who never had to shovel snow ,dig a ditch or cut the grass. He is currently middle aged, paid by wealthy coporations and persons to attack elected officials seeking to pass a Federal tax in any fashion because he feels, in addition to being remunerated for it,this is anathema to good governing. Congressmen in particular cow down to the non enforceable pledge they signed at his urging to garner favor ,brown nose points with"Conservatives" and their voting records who have flopped together like cow dung in a barn during a subzero winter in Montana. Hence,, brownnose.

It really is not NN (though he really is detestable) I am offended by but the elected personages in the Congress who took an oath of office that certainly overrides any oath to plump Noogie. Their job is to keep government financed with a prospect of a tomorrow for the present and future generations with no shutdowns or credit downgrades from the world. ,which is also in terrible fiscal status..

FURTHER; The election of the Teaparty Republicans if you can call them that,has presented America and the House of Reprehensibles with non realists who believe there is no consequence for American default and or standstill or at least some of them feel that way and House majority ``leader '' Boehner and weasel Cantor cannot or will not control them at the most inopportune times approaching at the end of Dec. or Jan. 1,2013.

The best hope is there will be a groundswell of votes against a substantial percentage of these non operative amateurs at governance so that there is hope AT THE START OF next year of a budget that does not condemn millions of downtrodden middle lower class people to sickness and even death while replenishing funds dedicated to the ranks of teachers, construction workers, police , firemen and research techs infrastructure and salaries. A GREAT CHANGEOVER MUST be made and the next election is in poker terms the ''ALL IN'' EFFORT, HOUSE,SENATE AND PRESIDENCY. MAKE NO MISTAKE !

FLIP THE VICTIM ,CLASS WARFARE.

Current propaganda from Republicans is similar to defense attorneys transforming the victim of a rape into the guilty party,"She wore sexy clothes","rubbed against him while dancing'' "made it seem she wanted it" etc.

Today Speaker Boehner , who yesterday could not get his caucus to support a bill to keep the government open with

3.7 billion dollars in appropriations for disaster flood relief, blamed the Democrats who seem to have a much better grip on the costs(exceeding eleven billion) for refusing to support the lowball number assigned in the bill written by the speaker of the house. So we may see another cliffhanger episode in Washington by Sept.30th.

This tactic has been employed on all matters where the GOP adopts Scrooge like numbers in fantasy situations blaming Democrats for the results of flamingly ignorant decisions made years ago by the bush administration such as cutting taxes for superrich individuals and corporations while passing unbalanced budgets ,HIDDEN COSTS UNDERTHE COUNTER, and fostering unpaid for wars with unprepared armed forces .(forcing our soldiers to face three to six tours in wars they could never win).

The GOP charge of Obama waging "class warfare "with a plan to return to tax rates from the Clinton era is another example of the urinal calling the kettle black. Or flipping., The Reagan administration tax code revision and bush with his "tax cuts"during wartime certainly established 2 classes diminishing the middle class while adding almost 300% more income to the"wealthy class"and less than 20% to the so called middle class("muddled") since 1970.Seems out of balance even to non accountants. 99 to one.

Tax cuts have built the deficit far more than spending.. Responsibility is not the Republicans' forte..And now I ask you to fast forward to March 2012 to take note of the following news items announced this week.

China announces a spending hike of11.2 percent in defense spending to $110,000 Billion dollars.Who is going to attack them- my question arises, WE KNOW America will not.

In comparison the US Congress,some of whom have been critical of President Obama's administration for REDUCING the Pentagon budget by 43 Billion dollars,has approved 662 Billion dollars, my calculator tells me that is 600% higher than the Chinese.And we are in the process of losing or withdrawing our forces of war from two area where "insurgents" held their own positions and countries for 9 years against the United States.THE ENEMY IS ON HOME TERRITORYH without an Air force, Navy, Long range rockets, armored vehicles, modern electronics, uniforms, - using robes, sandals, used Toyota pickup trucks ,weapons from 40 years ago and no medical care.

And we have in storage 10,000 Atomic bombs at a cost of Trillions. Not to be critical but.... And Republicans are complaining that President Obama is planning further cuts in the military?

The United States spends as much and more than all the nations in the world annually on war goods and manpower spread out over 167 nations. OUR PRIORITIES ARE DISASTER controlled by THE MIC !

MAILED ON APRIL FOOLS DAY !

To; the President, Democratic Congressmen and Senators of New Jersey

April 1,2012

I JUST WATCHED SIXTY MINUTES TEAR THE DEMOCRATIC ADMINISTRATION APART.QUICKLY.

My wife and I tuned in on Sunday night along with some other millions of viewers popular"60 minutes"and in 20 minutes we saw an article on Brevard County,FL that has turned into a plastic Dustbowl of unemployment and misery for the Space workers that lived high on the hog for thirty years while serving their country as the reporter said and images of space shots and flags waving in better years .They announces Obama promised when campaigning in the area that Florida Space industry jobs would continue but he was blamed for cutting them and Congress cut them all the more. Guess who "60" and those interviewed blamed?

Then came the "NEWS" spot stating gasoline pump prices went up 19 cents per gallon in a month and 1.60 in a year. Obama's fault.?

Immediately following was the announcement this week Japan lowered their corporate tax SO AMERICA now has the highest rate in the world at 39%(not mentioning that many of our slippery companies pay zero like GE and the average is less than 20% and many pay nothing.

Is there any one working on counter pro PR for this admin-istration who can watch over the national networks and see why in 20 minutes Obama and admistration can be made to look like Doctor Evil with no counter punching to relieve the impact? There has to be some concerted effort to reverse attack on these brief but constant articles that have an overlay of negativity. We get enough of this from Foxedup News. Please tell me how your political people are countering this forever smearing of our brand . If this continues WE LOSE! AND SO DOES AMERICA.

Yours for Democrats,

Jack Doyle

historical. THE COST OF OUR UNUSED AND USELESS ATOMIC WEAPONS AS OF 1996 ADD 25% FOR 2012

AND WE USED TWO OF THEM OVER 70 YEARS AGO. TRANSLATED THIS IS CLOSE TO SEVEN TRILLION 300 BILLION DOLLARS AND MORE SINCE A CONSTANT 1996 DOLLAR HAS DEPRECIATED

Total: $5,821.0 billion

in billions of constant 1996 dollars

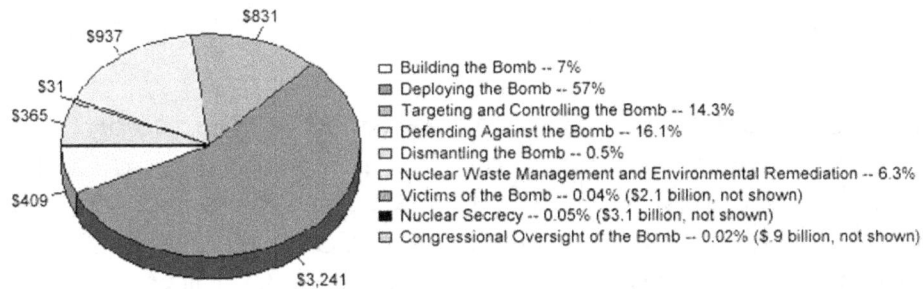

$831
$937
$31
$365
$409
$3,241

□ Building the Bomb -- 7%
▥ Deploying the Bomb -- 57%
▦ Targeting and Controlling the Bomb -- 14.3%
□ Defending Against the Bomb -- 16.1%
□ Dismantling the Bomb -- 0.5%
□ Nuclear Waste Management and Environmental Remediation -- 6.3%
▦ Victims of the Bomb -- 0.04% ($2.1 billion, not shown)
■ Nuclear Secrecy -- 0.05% ($3.1 billion, not shown)
□ Congressional Oversight of the Bomb -- 0.02% ($.9 billion, not shown)

*Includes average projected future-year costs for nuclear weapons dismantlement and fissile materials disposition and environmental remediation and waste management. Total actual and estimated expenditures through 1996 were $5,481.1 billion.

Source: *Atomic Audit: The Costs and Consequences of U.S. Nuclear Weapons Since 1940* (Brookings Institution Press, 1998)

I WAS ONCE DESCRIBED AS THE LAST ANGRY MAN!

Now here are millions holding the same views as I. Allow me to point out Occupy Wall Street, Oakland, Ca, Boston, Ma. Washington, D.C. and many other cities nation and worldwide are now part of what is typical of the ``mad as hell" attitude that I used to be accused of. This movement has been brought to a head in the past 6 months and depicts partially what I have felt about American Exceptionalism ,a favorite acclaim of the right wingers here. .America as a whole has been `` exceptionally IDIOTIC "over the past decade in so many ways and the demonstrators have "had it".

People who hear me think I am denigrating America when I say for instance ``we haven't won a war since the second world war "but how stupid are those who would argue? "Exceptionally ignorant "Idiots.   LOOK AT THEHEADLINES EACH DAY".

The new phrase of CNBC commentators puts it clearly `` you are entitled to your own opinion but not your own facts". The major problem is semantics, for example what is a win? Is it when the chief executive of a nation depicts it as such? Or when a banner hoisted over a war ship declaims it? While hundreds die and lose homes in all nations involved each week?

Common sense definition will say it is when soldiers from the nations at war and citizens of same are not killing each other or planning to do so. Iraq and Afghanistan cannot be so described, even after TEN YEARS .Any one arguing is "exceptionally ignorant". Or "thinking with their wishful"

As this is written the Port of Oakland ,California has been closed by OWS demonstrators costing millions of dollars to the American economy DAILY..Right or wrong this shows the strength and power of this movement and tactics they can employ .Meanwhile back at the ranch 12 of the chosen non functioning geniuses from Congress are about 23 days from reaching a non agreement on lowering over ten years a fifteen trillion dollar deficit, which equals about EIGHT TIMES our annual national gross product.

One of the reasons this agreement is almost impossible is due to the intransigence of the Republicans on the com-mittee all of whom have signed a Mickey Mouse "pledge" fostered by a political effete snob gadfly who has never held an elected office,was raised in wealth and associ-ated for decades with more than a dozen groups seeking the most they can drain out of the American people and economy with the least investment. I speak of Americans for Tax Reform, the US Chamber of Commerce, the National Rifle Association,and others with lobbying behind them. This omnipresent individual is Grover (Nuttwist)Norquist who receives at least a quarter of a million dollars per year for a part time position at Americans for Tax Reform which basically should have the words``for tax evasion" in their title.

Another interesting view of Nuttwist is he is involved in Muslim causes because he is married to an Arab woman of wealth and influence. His income from those causes is not known and he has managed to keep this part of his life well disguised. Occupy Wall Street People hold this man and other like him in contempt for his irresponsible self aggrandizing influence on benefits to the top 1% earners at greatest cost to the majority of citizens of America. Me too.

The New York Times today had an article showing that 280 of the top earning corporations in the United States paid only 18 ½% income tax for the past three years,not the corporate published rate of 35%.THREE YEARS! No friggin wonder we're broke.

Information such as this proves the crying and yammering by the right wing Republicans about how our corporations are "fighting with one hand tied behind them" against competitors abroad is a deliberate gross lie. Twenty five percent of the 280 firms owed less than ten percent in taxes. Over ten percent owed NOTHING 000000. Boeing and General Electric paid nothing, GE had a tax credit of over 3 Billion dollars. Corporate taxes represented only 1.3% of gross domestic product opposed to 6% during the 1950's.

Grover Nuttwist is still complaining that the US code taxes profits made abroad.

Boo Hoo,the facts are 67% of the firms doing any significant business overseas paid more in foreign taxes than to the

American treasury.``Occupy'' people are not tax experts but the Congress that represents them have accountants by the thousands .Loopholes need changes and complete discard so that all large corporations are on an even keel.

When will that happen? Not with this Congress.

How does the Peeparty not see this as essential and necessary?

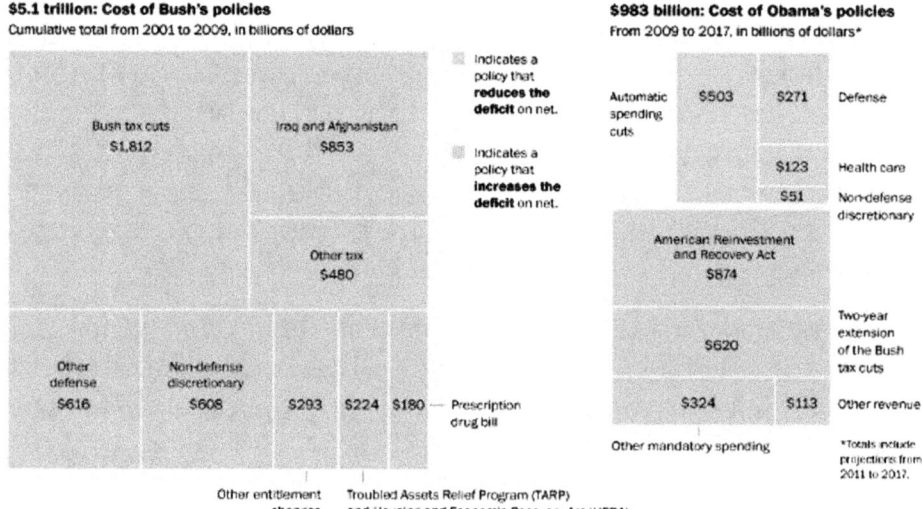

$5.1 trillion: Cost of Bush's policies
Cumulative total from 2001 to 2009, in billions of dollars

$983 billion: Cost of Obama's policies
From 2009 to 2017, in billions of dollars*

(Graph: Todd Lindeman/Ezra Klein; data: Center on Budget and Policy Priorities)

If we take the blackmailed 600Billion from the Obama share chart and place it where it belongs with Bush 's disasterous planning It is evident that Republicans spent 1000% more than Obama in about 96months versus 36 months for Obama.Unfortunatlely the Tax cuts were a continuing cancer on the economy with no jobs payout.

MONDAY, APR 9, 2012 7:30 AM EASTERN DAYLIGHT TIME

<u>The causes of the financial crisis</u>

A Wall Street insider explains how Greenspan contributed to the mortgage crisis and how to restore economic sanity

BY <u>SOPHIE ROELL</u>, <u>THE BROWSER</u>

Alan Greenspan (Credit: Reuters/Kevin Lamarque)

TOPICS:<u>THE BROWSER</u>, <u>BOOKS</u>, <u>WALL STREET</u>, <u>GREAT RECESSION</u>

This interview first appeared in The Browser, as part of the FiveBooks series. Previous contributors include Paul Krugman, Woody Allen and Ian McEwan. For a daily selection of new article suggestions and FiveBooks interviews, check out <u>The Browser</u> or follow <u>@TheBrowser</u> on Twitter.

Wall Street money manager Barry Ritholtz diagnoses the ills of America's political and economic system in a fizzing, irreverent analysis (with promised f-bombs thrown in).

I originally thought we were going to be talking about Wall Street today. But I got the sense from some of your book choices that one of the biggest offenders wasn't based on Wall Street at all, but on Constitution Avenue in Washington, D.C.

When you get bit by a dog, you don't just look at the dog, you have to look at the owner who is holding the leash. To me, a lot of the regulatory changes, and a lot of what the Federal Reserve did, stand on their own as a major factor. But if you've read David Hume, if you've studied the philosophy of causation, you have to look at what motivated those changes. I have these debates with friends. One group blames everything on big government; the other group blames everything on big corporations. The sad news is that there's really no difference between the two: Big government and big corporations work hand-in-hand. If you want to know who is the puppet and who is the puppet master, it sure looks like Wall Street has been pulling the strings of Congress for many, many, many years.

But the Federal Reserve itself should be insulated from those kinds of pressures.

They should be, except in the person of Alan Greenspan. He's just this gnarly mass of contradictions. He's an acolyte of Ayn Rand – believes that no intervention in free markets is the right approach – and yet he proceeded to spend his entire career, from 1987 through 2005, with his hands on the levers of Federal Reserve policy. He manipulated interest rates and money supply in order to win the love of traders. In 2001 he took rates down to unprecedented levels – below 2 percent – and kept them there for three years. Rates were at 1 percent for a full year! That had simply never occurred before in history. If you look at the late 1950s and early 1960s, rates would dip below 2 percent, but only for weeks at a time. In the "Who is to blame?" game Alan Greenspan is number one with the bullet, he's top of the list. You can't blame everything on him, but he's the one who let all the gas fumes into the enclosed warehouse, knowing that a bunch of smokers were coming in to have a cigarette. Taking rates down to irresponsibly low rates is what set the stage for everything that took place over the next decade.

Are you saying that just as Ben Bernanke <u>admitted</u> the Federal Reserve had caused the first Great Depression, this crisis can also be blamed on our central bank?

The world isn't black and white. We can't just say, "The butler did it." There were many causes, lots of poor judgements... The Federal Reserve was a significant element. But if you want to do it chronologically, you may want to go back further into the history. The bailout of Chrysler in 1980 set the stage. The rescue of Long Term Capital Management (LTCM) in 1998 encouraged a lot of moral hazard. Then there was all the radical deregulation, the undoing of some of the post-Depression rules that had operated so successfully for 75 years to prevent a major meltdown. The undoing of Glass-Steagall didn't cause the crisis, but it made it much worse. Then there was the Commodity Futures Monetization Act (CFMA) of 2000, which completely exempted derivatives from any oversight or regulation and removed all reserve requirements. These all built to set up a situation that was extremely dangerous. So maybe the fumes were already in the warehouse and Greenspan taking rates down to 1 percent was the spark that ignited the conflagration.

In 2008 an executive of a power company was paid 110 times as much money in one year as the president of the

United States of America. Supposedly he earned it no doubt according to terms of an employment contract.

Could this man possibly have contributed to his company more value than the leader of the "free world" does in a year to the entire planet? And do ball players who "work" for the Yankees baseball team really earn 10, 20 and 30 times more than the leader of the United States of America because they contribute more to mankind and the world?

The problem of disproportionate compensation is coming up more and more in the news and will eventually have to be regulated by a cap by industry and the government in some fashion because it has contributed to the downfall of America in many ways in the past half century.

A typical egregious example was the payment to the president of Reebok the sneaker company perhaps 20 years ago when he contractually bargained for and was paid on the "gross receipts" of the company after having transferred manufacturing to the far east and was able to price his goods low enough to enlarge sales massively .His pay exceeded $25 million dollars for one year, his contractual salary was less than one million but what a bonus. And this contract lasted for many years and was agreed to by the board.

Do sneaker sales justify such enrichment, not in a billion years. But such examples are now commonplace. What has FACEBOOK contributed to mankind ,the health and welfare of people in the world that justifies the billions of dollars that fall to the owner/ originators of the firm in less than ten years? Does it cure cancer?

Meanwhile salaries of American government elected officials are so low by industry , banking and investment market standards it is no wonder that graft and corruption are epidemic amongst those who must seek reelection at the will and whim of the people every few years. And yet voters rant against Congressional pay rates with no concept of equity.

Of course considering the2010 -2012 Congress with an approval rating at or belowTEN PERCENT 10% BY EVERY POLL THEIR ANGER IS UNDERSTANDABLE ,... but get this------

The House of Reprehensibles just passed a jobs bill, the first since they formed under the aegis of the tea party and Weasels Cantor and Blowhard. They also passed a bill addressing China's subsidies on exports to America of several products which was drawn up by the Obama administration. This is NO DOUBT BECAUSE THE ELECTION IS NEARING and the polls are useful AND FORCEFUL although they do not ask if respondents hold which party responsible , a GLARING MISTAKE.

The polling firms know there are just 2 parties in Clowngress, why not include the questions by D or R?

PEE PARTY CULT INCREASES BORROWING COSTS FOR DELUDED FLOCK.(and all of us) August 2011.

So Standard and Poors will make us all poorer according to the common knowledge of many by downgrading the United States credit standing by a notch below triple A.

Using any credit arrangement ,a business loan, purchasing a car ,house ,refrig ,and everything on time will cost Americans more in the future and we can thank the unrelenting pressure from the Peeparty pack of morons who were willing to have the nation default,the Democratic leaders and Republican leaders who believed they would and President Obama who would not pursue the 14th Amendment strategy. Many learned people in government,scholars including President Clinton felt that should have been the solution to a standoff that should never have reached a 72 hour brink when the predicament was based on a Neanderthal fictional mechanism crafted in 1917.

Remember the Republican party and Fox news bestowed this polyglot abortion of politics on the country and make no mistake about it.The same GOP is also sorry now that the reality has shit the fan.

The monstrosity forced on the President and the nation will succeed in helping drag the economy down bringing the poor and middle class to an even lower rung on the ladder of life no matter whether the 12 wise men come up with a"compromise" or the draconian guillotine falls on all of us -.and the rich will get richer,make no mistake.

FOX NEWS SHOWS WHAT THE ENTIRE CORPORATION IS WORLDWIDE BY SCANDAL IN ENGLAND

Rupert Murdoch THIS WEEK is closing the most circulated tabloid newpaper in Great Britian.. The prior appointment of the editor of that paper to a high position in the Cameron government indicates the type of influence Rupert's minions exert on politics there and worldwide including of course the USA. Here they just have not been caught in something illegal as yet .This demonstrates how perilous a dishonest news organization to a nation and its' citizens can be.

But the fact is they are after power for power's sake- it's not just money it's to embellish the Murdock empire at the expense of truth in press and media always exerting right-ward dictatorial influence for corporate riches and never to benefit the populace as a whole. This is true worldwide .

Closing the tabloid News of the World is just a desperate effort on the part of this grasping corporation to maintain respectability as a true purveyor of the news while pursuing the takeover of Sky Broadcasting, a twelve billion dollar deal for the largest pay TV company in England which has been in preparation for months. The terrible odor of the tapped phone calls to hundreds and bribes to police and the gross appearance of illegal prostituting of all of these entities can kill this massive profitable deal. Needless to say Robber Rupert will expend much capital and:"pull" to dig out of the muck and stay in contention for this prize.

Murdock is a world low class (ask his former wife) bastard and perhaps the most dangerous independent corporation to all of us in America.The disentanglement of this phone tapping ,bribery and illegal governmental influence in England will extend to America as well ,just watch- Rupert is a great pal to the Republican party and the machinations of his corporate tentacles have already done vast harm in the US. Remember his Foxed Newscorp is an import thanks to Noot Getrich and it brought a disease of calumny and deceit that spread since it came into the country.

In 1811, two years after Jefferson left the Presidency, Jefferson wrote a letter to General Thaddeus Kosciuszko, a hero of the American Revolution. Jefferson said that he supported taxes (then tariffs, since there was no income tax yet) falling entirely on the wealthy. As Jefferson explained: "The farmer will see his government supported, his children educated, and **the face of this country made a paradise by the contributions of the rich alone,** without his being called on to spend a cent from his earnings."

Here is someone else who was an outspoken proponent of progressive taxation: Adam Smith, who literally "wrote the book" on capitalism. In 1776, in *The Wealth of Nations*, Smith wrote:

"The necessaries of life occasion the great expense of the poor. They find it difficult to get food, and the greater part of their little revenue is spent in getting it. **The luxuries and vanities of life occasion the principal expense of the rich,** and a magnificent house embellishes and sets off to the best advantage all the other luxuries and vanities which they possess. A tax upon house-rents, therefore, would in general fall heaviest upon the rich; and in this sort of inequality there would not, perhaps, be anything unreasonable. **It is not very unreasonable that the rich should contribute to the well being of all** "

TEAPARTY ORIGINS, SICK MINDS UNEDUCATED NON THINKERS.

The Teaparty exploded into being by claiming that Obama's mildly Keynesian stimulus of $787 billion was anti-American and Socialist. We had lost nearly 3 million jobs the previous year, we lost 741,000 in the month that Obama was inaugurated, and the economy was free-falling into a Depression. Even Republican economists contended that the U.S. desperately needed a Keynesian infusion to stop the economy from spiraling into an abyss. But somehow in contradiction to every thinking economist and Secretary Paulson's earlier palsied balls less plan it was horribly wrong to save the nation from reliving 1933. On the basis of this absurd position every House Republican voted against Obama's stimulus and the Tea Party subsequently won a tremendous political windfall -- which has made the Republican Party more extreme than ever.

The Tea Party is overwhelmingly white, middle-class, and either middle-aged or elderly. It thrives on a deeply felt dichotomy between the deserving and the undeserving. At the grassroots level, much of the Tea Party is not hostile to Social Security or Medicare, unlike the professional ideologues that are exploiting it. Tea Party Republicans are quite certain that they deserve their own Social Security and Medicare. But they are outraged that undeserving people get taxpayer-funded benefits from the government. In the Tea Party version of the American dream, there is no such thing as the common good. There is only the sum of individual goods, which many people do not deserve.

The Right-wing anti-Obama literature charges incessantly that white liberals coddled an undeserving Obama into and through Harvard Law School, financed his political career, and fawned over him all the way to the White House, where he betrays America's national interests and slathers the undeserving with Obamacare and food stamps. The Tea Party, a new phenomenon, capitalizes on resentments and a mean-spirited ideology that are far from new in U.S. American life.

But the idea that we owe obligations to each other to serve the common good is equally long-standing in American history and politics. A federal budget is a moral document. If we scaled back America's global military empire and reinstated a morally decent tax system and budget, we could eliminate the entire federal debt by 2021 without cutting Social Security, Medicare, Medicaid, education, or research.

A decent system would have additional brackets for the highest incomes, as the U.S. once did. It would have a bracket for $1 million earners and a bracket for $10 million dollar earners and a bracket for $100 million earners and so on. It would lift the cap on the regressive Social Security tax, taxing salaries above $110,000 per year. It would tax capital gains as ordinary income. It would cap the benefit on itemized deductions at 28 percent. It would tax U.S. foreign income as it is earned. It would eliminate the subsidies for oil, gas, and coal companies. It would place a tax on credit default swaps and futures and charge a leverage tax on the megabanks.

These are not radical proposals. If we adopted all of them, we would still be well below European levels of taxation. All of them together merely, mildly restore the principle that people should pay taxes on the basis of their ability to do so -- a principle that polls very well even in red states.

Gary Dorrien is Reinhold Niebuhr Professor of Social Ethics at Union Theological Seminary and Professor of Religion at Columbia University. His 16 books include "<u>Kantian Reason and Hegelian Spirit</u>" (Wiley-Blackwell, 2012) and the recently published "<u>The Obama Question: A Progressive Perspective</u>" (Rowman & Littlefield).

This Blogger's Books *from* amazon.com.

A FEDERAL BUDGET IS A MORAL DOCUMENT.

If we scaled back America's global military empire and reinstated a morally decent tax system and budget, we could eliminate the entire federal debt by 2021 without cutting Social Security, Medicare, Medicaid, education, or research.

A decent system would have additional brackets for the highest incomes, as the U.S. once did. It would have a bracket for $1 million earners and a bracket for $10 million dollar earners and a bracket for $100 million earners and so on. It would lift the cap on the regressive Social Security tax, taxing salaries above $110,000 per year. It would tax capital gains as ordinary income. It would cap the benefit on itemized deductions at 28 percent. It would tax U.S. foreign income as it is earned. It would eliminate the subsidies for oil, gas, and coal companies. It would place a tax on credit default swaps and futures and charge a leverage tax on the megabanks.

These are not radical proposals. If we adopted all of them, we would still be well below European levels of taxation. All of them together merely, mildly restore the principle that people should pay taxes on the basis of their ability to do so -- a principle that polls very well even in red states.

Gary Dorrien is Reinhold Niebuhr Professor of Social Ethics at Union Theological Seminary and Professor of Religion at Columbia University. His 16 books include "Kantian Reason and Hegelian Spirit" (Wiley-Blackwell, 2012) and the recently published "The Obama Question: A Progressive Perspective" (Rowman & Littlefield).

This Blogger's Books *from* **amazon**.com.

More in Politics...

LETTER TO STAR LEDGER, NEWARK, NJ

Worst of Christie Back in Spades (CHRISTY Whitman started this mess) Oct. 1, 2010

Think back to the Christie Whitman debacle when everyday NJ expenses were bonded without public permission,the state borrowed to fund pension funds and EZ pass doubled in cost under her administration. Her Husband and campaign manager made money on it.

The Rest of the Story is not only is New Jersey afflicted with another Republican Christie CATERING TO HIS WEALTHY CLIENTELE SUPPORTERS who considers the EPA and environment a nuisance but he is arrogant enough to insist on tax cuts for the richest people in the state and is willing to defund promised homestead rebates for the senior community as well as contributions to workers retirement funds in the state. This is in order to afford a NEW MASSIVE affront to equity and good government.

Since the rich are not like you and me it is no wonder the Republican establishment is seeking him as a "rockstar" for candidates like Meg Wealthy Whitman (another one) California governor hopeful with half a billion in personal fortune in her pocket already.

Instead of staying home in New Jersey as a new governor who has a bundle of debt, a deficit of double the NJ State budget in pension contributions he is traveling helping a near billionaire seek funds and election in California which has a deficit five times as large as the Garden State. You know,this is the" Kel iforn ia "where the departing GOP governor with The Jay Leno "occent" promised to solve all ills WHEN RUNNING FOR OFFICE years back and suddenly it was not a happy movie ending but a disaster) His legacy is deficit ,divorce and a walking talking mistake of unthinking sexual deceit, AN ILLEGITIMATE SON.

By the time our New Jersey Governor "Rockstar" ended his first year we will have no funding for roads, bridges or highways, will have lost millions in Highway funds from the US Treasury already commited AND SPENT! Also there is another FOUR HUNDRED MILLION in educational funds already lost due to Governor Christie's blunders and obstinacy with his appointed ,then fired, Education executive Schundler.THE FALL GUY! And highway repairs and roadwork will be shutdown - again thanks to our new "Bully "traveling rockstar.

And every village, Town and municipality in our State is losing Teachers, Police, Firemen and essential services due to this" governor".

Is this a "rockstar" or a rockhead ? Will the duped citizens vote him in again? Or seek to impeach him?

Jack Doyle

ISSA'T AN OVERSIGHT,3 TIMES ARRESTED FOR CAR THIEF AND ILLEGALGUNS

- As Chairman of the full committee, Rep. Issa may serve as an ex *officio* member of all subcommittees

- **Committee on the Judiciary**

- Subcommittee on Commercial and Administrative Law

- Subcommittee on Courts and Competition Policy

- Republican Study Committee

Obama administration

After becoming Chairman of the Committee on Oversight and Government Reform, Issa has become a vocal advocate for investigations into the Obama administration, including the TARP and Financial Crisis Inquiry Commission, corruption in Afghanistan, Wikileaks, and the FDA, among other issues.[34] On March 22, 2011, it was reported that he accused the administration of retaliating against Catherine Papoi, who complained the administration was blocking public access to records.[35]

Criticism and controversy

9/11

In April 2008, the *Daily News* reported that Issa had said that the federal government "'just threw' buckets of cash at New York for an attack 'that had no dirty bomb in it, it had no chemical munitions in it.'"[36] He was also reported as having asked "why the firefighters who went there and everybody in the city of New York needs to come to the federal government for the dollars versus this being primarily a state consideration."[36] In September 2009, Issa's office released a statement indicating that his comments had been misrepresented and that the questions he asked concerned unpassed bill H.R. 3543, which, according to that statement "would give U.S. taxpayer dollars to those who did not suffer physical injury and did not work at or around Ground Zero."[37][38]

Letter to businesses

Following the 2010 elections, Issa sent a letter to more than 150 trade associations, companies and think tanks, asking them to tell him which existing and proposed regulations would harm job growth.[39] Liberal critics have charged that Issa was "embracing regulatory capture."[40] Elijah Cummings, the ranking member of the House Committee on Oversight and Government Reform, said Issa's letters were tantamount to "inviting businesses to tell us what they want us to do as opposed to protecting the American people."[41]

REFERENCES

1. ∧ Montopoli, Brian. (November 6, 2009). <u>237 Millionaires in Congress.CBS News</u>.

2. ∧ <u>"Personal Finances — Net Worth, 2008"</u>. *opensecrets. org*; <u>Center for Responsive Politics</u>.

3. ∧ **<u>a</u> <u>b</u> <u>c</u> <u>d</u> <u>e</u> <u>f</u> <u>g</u> <u>h</u> <u>i</u> <u>j</u> <u>k</u> <u>l</u> <u>m</u> <u>n</u> <u>o</u> <u>p</u> <u>q</u> <u>r</u> <u>s</u> <u>t</u> <u>u</u> <u>v</u> <u>w</u> <u>x</u> <u>y</u>** <u>Lizza, Ryan</u> (January 24, 2011).<u>"Don't Look Back"</u>. *The New Yorker*. Retrieved January 20, 2011.

4. ∧ Broder, David S. (December 21, 1997). <u>"California's Battle of the Bankbooks"</u>. *<u>The Washington Post</u>*.

THE BANKING STYSTEM OF THE UNITED STATES OF AMERICA

Bernie Sanders, Senator who really represents the people rather than a party as he states INDEPENDENT in his mast-head , literature and on the ballot at the polling booth has looked carefully at the FEDERAL RESERVE ,members and affiliations .I am shocked at the revelations in his report of Oct.2011. Hence the above titled segment of this report recommended to those of you who purchase this book.

DUMBOCRACY ENVISIONED by Carl Rove , THE HOAX OF VOTER FRAUD

A glaring lack in the US Democratic system is the lack of incentive for citizens to cast votes diluting the good and promoting the bad in governance.

More than a dozen states have passed laws in Republican legislatures through various subterfuges like requiring a photographic" voter card" or a birth certificate by those casting a vote. These new "voter fraud" laws seek to disenfranchise the poor and elderly, college students and the young who have difficulty in accessing such documents.

The pretext of voter fraud is FRAUD ITSELF as there is no evidence of

more than a few dozen illegally cast votes in any elections in all covered voting districts over the past decade.

A real fraud was the appointment of one W. bush to be President of the United States of America by his dad's appointed buddy to the?Supreme ?Court. No favoritism there?

This concerted ID card effort like a poll tax is directed by Carl Rove to prevent Democratic votes now and in the future. A voter who does not drive must pay a lot to get an ID in,time off fromwork,photo,etc. The Federal election commission now is seeking to overturn these transparent efforts to control elections.

Some nations like Australia have a penalty for not voting and get a participation rate in the 90 percentile. The threat of a small fine equal to a traffic ticket brought voting participation to that figure and higher in two election cycles of 2 years.

In a less dictatorial America we could give an incentive of tax credits for voting in National and state elections increasing them after for instance 5 continuous votes, then ten, etc. Such a plan would encourage more interest in candidates' views and keep voters up on the promises made and kept in selected election campaigns as time goes on.

Participative Democracy is badly needed here as witness the majority of citizens until late 2008 thought that Saddam

Hussein had responsibility for the Twin Towers destruction, also that we had found weapons of mass destruction in Iraq.

FOX News doing their work of fabrication.

Such ignorance is unconscionable except for the fact that the Republican administration propaganda machine deliberately kept these myth alive for as long as they could including outright lying whenever possible.,for obvious reasons.

While I'm at it with reference to faults in American democracy the Jury system is another problem that needs attention that no one in authority is willing to give it.

Adversary proceedings with`` winner take all" thrust (guilty or not guilty) encourage prosecutors to withhold evidence, coach witnesses to lie and simply adopt a winner take all attitude and the same holds true for poorly paid defense councils who are many times appointed by law to the " indigent." This cost US(Us Suckers) HUGE BUCKS.

In many cases the truth is not in them nor is it sought. Juries do not have the technical knowledge they need to settle and adjudicate complicated scientific and medical cases and must rely on evidence without referring to further study or testimony of unbiased scientists ,doctors or specialists etc. who have no self interested point to make. They are in all cases paid by one side or the other and dueling experts confuse jurors.

Juries cannot question witnesses or dueling attorneys.

The Menendez Brothers and O.J. Simpson trials in California were a perfect example of the twisting of justice because juries were subpar in performance intellectually. Defense attorneys seek to empanel near ignorance while prosecutors "settle" for maybe the appearance of some intellect.

Many Countries have trial by a jury of jurists, judges who know the law and can ask questions at appropriate times which jurors can not .All courtroom actors are educated to their task . Justice and the truth represent the public interest though the defense will take the side that makes the defendant look innocent as much as possible.

Another poorly thought out facet of our justice system is the election of judges based on advertising and campaigns by the candidates who in many county (parish) or local cases do not have to have any legal education whatsoever .They can be tailors, mechanics or farmers and as long as they say the pleasing(politic) thing in their campaigns and get enough votes and then ;

"HERE COME THE JUDGE."

And then here's a legal situation that will make you proud,

A recent case that was a miscarriage of justice had to be brought to the Supreme Court to make it right. Even there the case was close, the decision was split 5 to 4 .It involved a suit in the West Virginia supreme court Chief Justice Brennan presiding. Brennan after having benefited from THREE MILLION DOLLARS spent on advertising advocating his reelection by the defendant Massey Coal in the case not recusing himself from a decision threw out a FIFTY MILLION DOLLAR award to be paid by Massey to the plaintiff coal companies who were harmed by fraud by the big spending Massey defendant.

Sadly most Americans are unaware that KING COAL - THE ASTHMA INDUCER IS SEEKING TO RULE THE LAND led by the self seeking greedy Koch Brothers, multibillion dollar corporation.

The sophistry of the claim that the first amendment supporting free speech as it has only recently been interpreted by the corporately controlled United States Supreme Court enables advertising for candidates for any office and in this case a judge as long as that service is not paid by the candidate. This masquerade makes free speech an expansive WEALTH DRIVEN right of the wealthiest as opposed to a small group of 2 or 200 people who can only afford a dollar per person while another can spend millions through "focus groups" or facades of any kind.They "focus'all right. Spelled with FU—us.

Exceptionalism at work in all its' glory.

CANARIES IN THE MINE Expiring from lack of Truth and a poisoned atmosphere .

It is predictable that two of the wives of the "Supremes" are members of organizations that might be considered right wing to the extreme but they are open about it. . Arrogant. In some nations this would render their husbands ineffective as arbiters of what is right and just and they would be expelled as judges in whatever court they presided. But here the wives are "exercising their constitutional rights" sharing their charms and pillows and America reeks of the stench of the corporate lackeys that control the most important court in the nation.

This corporate leaning five Catholic clique headed up by a man whose wife is an important member of a group dedicated to defeating the law that grants a woman's right to choose regarding abortion also has the wife of Justice Thomas who is a member of the rightwing "Liberty Central"segment of the " Pee Party" I quickly learned to despise. Me and Jon Stewart.

195

If you don't think this has the odor of corporate corruption your olfactory sense of fairness and equity is severely limited. The glaring example - Look at the 2nd Amendment, since this group has assumed control the" militia" requirement for bearing of arms has been rendered a non factor .Everyone can bear arms and they can be purchased like candy at a confectionary store or donuts at a bakery.

And the right of free speech and massive monetary control of media has been granted to corporations as if they were individuals and their billions are outspending any groups of citizens who desire to help a party or candidate win an election that works against the corporate interests And all of this in the past two years or less. Old "KING COAL" with fifty billion on hand in the Koch Brothers treasury is a propaganda machine that can kill truth and the two party system in America.

Here are the limited words of the First Amendment,simple and to the point-

Congress shall make no law respecting an establishment of religion, or prohibiting the free exercise thereof; or abridging the freedom of speech, or of the press; or the right of the people peaceably to assemble, and to petition the Government.

And our current high court , high on arrogance, has rendered the poor peasants speechless while the lords of greed pass legal interpretations dripping with monetary advantages and favoritism to wealthy interests. And the canaries are dying.

DESPERATE TIMES CALL FOR THE BIG LIE AND OFTEN. GOEBBELS ALL OVER AGAIN.

Randy Rudy Giuliani famously asserted in a speech recently that during the Bush administration there had been no attempts at terrorism on American soil .

The audacious aim of such a fallacious statement was that there would be some people eager to feel friendly to this failed presidency or anxious to feel good about Republicans in general who would forget unconsciously that Sept 11th, 2001 and the World Trade Center/Pentagon attacks were 9 months into Bush rule and that he had been warned about Osama Bin Laden and his plan to attack the US.

To further the lie the episodes of the Richard Reid 'shoe bomber" and anthrax dissemination in our mails to government officials were also conveniently forgotten.

Would anyone suspect a concerted public CON JOB on the part of a group like the Republican hierarchy such as Rove, Giuliani, and the like?

Please, take a look at the clowns running for president on the R side in 2012.What a collection of self seeking conceited liars. For the most part because they are involved in a primary they must appeal to various interests and intellectual levels in states that have less than an educated populace ,Iowa ,S. Carolina, Rhode Island as starters .SO THE CLOWNS WILL SAY ANYTHING TO CATER AND PATRONIZE THE LOWING cattle-sheeple masses to get the nomination from this fanatic minority,THE BASE.

They will lie now and apologize or"skate" later . The mormon candidates have a difficult time explaining their "faith" and luckily this subject has not come up in the debates but it will later in the minds of many far right evangelist voters.

PERTINENT INFO FOR ECONOMIC HISTORY
HOW THE U.S. (US SUCKERS) GOT SHAFTED

John McCain,the GOP 2008 candidate for president had Phil Gramm as his closest economic counselor.Inthe past when Gramm was a senator from Texas, he was the prime Republican force pushing through the Gramm-Leach-Bliley Act. It repealed the old Glass-Steagall Act, passed in the Great Depression, which prohibited a commercial bank from being in the investment and insurance business. President Bill Clinton cheerfully signed it into law. Asleep and duped.

A year later Gramm, chairman of the Senate Banking Committee, attached a 262-page amendment to an omnibus appropriations bill, voted on by Congress right before a recess. The amendment received no scrutiny and duly became the Commodity Futures Modernization Act which okayed deregulation of investment banks, exempting most over the counter derivatives, credit derivatives, credit defaults, and swaps from regulatory scrutiny. Thus were born the scams that produced the debacle of Enron, a company on whose board sat Gramm's wife Wendy. She had served on the Commodity Futures Trading Commission from 1983 to 1993 and devised many of the rules coded into law by her husband in 2000. She should have baked cookies and knitted at home for the good of the nation.

Somewhat stained by the Enron debacle Gramm quit the senate in 2002 and began to enjoy the fruits of his own deregulatory efforts. He became a vice chairman of the giant Swiss bank UBS' new investment arm in the US, lobbying Congress, the Federal Reserve and the Treasury Department about banking and mortgage issues in 2005 and 2006, urging Congress to roll back strong state rules trying to crimp the predatory tactics of the subprime mortgage industry. UBS took a bath of about $20 billion in write offs from bad real estate loans this year.""

Gramm's the real Richard III of the lending/finance/GSE scam, though Clinton may be just as responsible, given his signature. As this is posted the Republicans always eager to prove that no errors were ever made allowing free rein to banks are now fighting the new Dodd/Frank regulations for banks but a TWO BILLION DOLLAR LOSS BY THE HUGE JP MORGAN INSTITUTION this week proves how desperately oversight and closer government regulations and overseers are needed. Chairman Jamie Dimond"s bluster and hyperbole will not bring back TWO BILLION BUCKS for depositors or prevent future defalcations. It happened under his watch and he was paid with a fifty percent increase in 2011 Twenty one Million dollars.! Imagine if they had paid him less?

But he is a handsome devil sent from Central Casting to play the part. Worth every penny? JAMIE IS AGAINST THE VOLCKER RULE! HOORA FOR US BANKS .....

IN AMERICA IT IS NOT WHAT THINGS ARE - IT IS WHAT THEY SEEM AS DESCRIBED BY FOX NEWS.

Current so-called "rock star" Corpulent Christie, 2 years into his term as governor of New Jersey spoke yesterday at the Reagan library purporting to be an expert in all things foreign and domestic about the problems this nation is having. Hearkening back to Reagan's success(?) in curing all problems during his presidency this pompous tool of the wealthy seemed to intimate he could follow in his footsteps with similar result in Jersey or perhaps in the nation should he deign to run for president.

Since his oratory was a speech and not a debate his words fell on ears eager to accept all he claimed and the audience with an estimated multimillion dollar each net worth ate it up. If it was foie gras they would have been surfeited and left looking like their adored speaker , THE BULLY..

The fact that during his short term in office this caterer to billionaires has decimated education in NJ and added to the poverty level in large areas in half of the population of New Jersey while protecting the lowered tax level of the wealthiest is not to be mentioned .Another "accomplishment" of his is condemning NJ commuters to downtown NYC to a single tube 100 years old because of reneging on an agreement to enlarge the system planned years ago by bipartisan leaders in the area While NJ Republicans run TV ad s claiming the gov has brought NJ back the StarLedger shows a headline stating one in four in the state are in Poverty!

IMAGINE IF THAT IS EXPLODED BY TERRORISTS ? THINK AHEAD GOV !

As expected Christie criticized the Obama administration plan to adjust higher tax levels for individuals earning a quarter of a million dollars per year saying the plan would "penalize" success. Of course, not mentioning that those levels existed after a tax increase passed by Reagan while in office. Forgetting that Reagan presided over the greatest percentage increase in U. S. deficit of 300% in his 8 years despite there were no wars - making the numbers 3 Trillion worth understanding.

It is no coincidence the Messiah like Christie was spirited out of New Jersey in Sept. for a secret (to the citizens of NJ) fund (R)raiser sponsored by those infamous propagators of ill health and pollution ,the Koch Brothers 50 Billion dollar fortuned owners of the largest coal conglomerate in America. Christie was the keynote speaker decrying teachers ,their unions and their desires that run contra his own. The facts are Christie acts like a monarch stating"reporters are not entitled to know everything I do".His BS speech before this illustrious group of the greedy was secretly taped by a columnist and reported in various newspapers as revealed by Milton Friedman.

With this kind of financing available suddenly new advertisements appear on TV in the metropolitan areas of NJ, NY, extolling the corpulent one's virtues and "accomplishments"again the puffery (BS)has no rebuttal as yet but it will appear. Minds are not always configured in the voting public's mind by one campaign. This can be seen in the recent saga of Texas governor six gun "Boots Perry" who even in the minds of Republicans is up and then down which is why the"thug from NJ' is in the run being implored by the corporate greedy group to"save" A NOMINATION which is non deserving.

Problem is; Despite all the observable facts the American scene was left in a 65 Trillion deficit by Republicans circa 2001- 2008 and all but one of the current candidates for office held to that party for a lifetime and the polluters and grasping monied groups of America are supporting them there are still votes in the poor and middle(muddled)class up for grabs as indicated by the midterm Congressional elections.

201

That gave rise to the Pee party (my appellation) whose leaders would rather the US Treasury default on all obligations or deficits since 1835 than compromise a solution. Further, presidential candidates who in no particular order deny global warming, evolution (science), , the Federal Reserve system ,Federal Health Care, Federal Education Involvement, Social Security ,outlaw the income tax ,would illegalize abortion and a host of other nightmare scenarios .And Fox News gives support and propaganda to this scourge that now is the excrement laden tail wagging the Republican cur. Speaker Blowhard no doubt would love to be rid of this group that has infected his disaffected "party".

IT'S BROKE WHEN YOU CAN'T FIX IT…..

During my early years in College sociology class the FAMOUS educational text "Cultural Lag" was a prime book to be studied and mulled over with thousands of examples and words. After that year in my life I almost never heard it. Most people if I mentioned it laughed and didn't know the meaning.

Since then it has proven to be a seriously operative phenomenon but in my opinion it should be renamed or postulated as" GOVERNMENTAL LEGISLATIVE LAG'' which would be more descriptive…or to put it in English "America is stuck in the 20thCentury".

Reason being it is not cultures that have lagged but the more serious and well financed governments of the world that have fallen behind in keeping civilization civil by not governing for the benefit of ALL.

Examples would be nations that permit their brain and brawn to abandon their native land and in turn those nations that permit encroachment that is unlimited to the detriment of their own citizens for decades. Such as Mexico and China with the United States as the offending enabler. The American people and government lose tremendously by sticking to the proverb enscribed on the Statue of Liberty now 160 years after it was written .. Asking for "tired huddled masses' implied legal immigrants who would blend in and contribute and be accounted for, not someone who would swim across a river or or a freighter from Macao or be smuggled at great personal cost by a criminal"coyote ".

So this is an example of "lag"that is causing America to bleed to death. Our legislative bodies over the years controlled by Republicans have placed emphasis on the spending of billions in "defense and security" funds on wars all over the globe, systems of protection against missiles that have not worked that can be defeated easily by false warheads against "frenemies"(I.E. Russia) who have no wherewithal or desire to attack the United States. We maintain alliances with false friends who are mendaciously corrupt since they were born hundreds of years ago - those we now favor and support in Iraq and Afghanistan.

Our depleted military can't control the border in Pakistan and we deal billions of dollars to corrupt officials in that nation . Nevertheless we allowed close to a million illegals to enter our Southern borders each year. When we place 10,000 national guard troops on duty there we do not allow them to apprehend or shoot any invaders in any way. Hundreds of thousands of troops in the middle east are engaged in wars that have lasted 8 years with no definite end..the upshot is we have an army of over 150,000 troops on assignment and are no more protected or safer than we were on Sept. 11, 2001.

How can any country afford free food and shelter,medical care and education to people who do not understand the adoptive language and provide them with free interpreters and attorneys to untangle their self induced problems.? And extend the protections of unearned citizenship during that time when natural born citizens are not so treated ?The answer is it,thatis WE CANNOT!

This brings me back to my original theme there have been politicians and groups within our political parties that have promoted behind America's back these very policies that are helping destroy us and our "borders". It's broke when you can't fix it and we can't fix the border in Pakistan or on our Southern borders of Texas, Arizona, California, Nevada, New Mexico or Florida.

Lobbyists for the ConAgra, Smithfield slaughterhouses, pickers and packers and big boxstores like Walmart have made sure our funds for border protection have been held at a low levels to provide illegals to keep labor costs low, profit levels high, this is all done in the dead of night in Washington,DC. visas are arranged for immigrants "temps"so called many of whom never go home.

The reasons we can't fix this seriously slow death dealing problem to our nation is we have no free will to do so .Free Will is considered a religious question or moral problem but reality can show you it is NOT! Ask yourself how many times have you learned from the newspapers, magazines or TV, Internet that over 60% of the population is not in favor of a war? Many times over the past 8 years - but we have no free will to discontinue such action because of previous decisions placing obligations on our form of government and the elected persons we put in charge of same.

Look at what Yalta did to us long ago! Our signatory President was dead but we had to abide and protect his agreements to maintain international credence and future stability.

Obama who would like nothing better than to get out of Iraq and Afghanistan has hastened the previous withdrawal dates for same but is stuck with critics in the military and Republican party.And worse, there is a danger in abandoning allies developed in the warring nations we invaded,when we disengage will they protect against our enemies or enable them to attack from their homestate and turn on us?And will they be eliminated by indigenous others?

Other countries like Canada , England, Japan France, all Scandanavian countries, have systems that can inject new people holding different ideas and plans into official power much faster on important issues holding more frequent elections by a vote of "no confidence"..But this is not the crux of the free will problem.Nor the solution.

The power in government now comes from accumulated monies by corporations or wealthy individuals and families who have taken 90% of the wealth of America and integrated it into their own beneficial packages through politics and religion. Recent analysis reveals they number only 13,000 families who to repeat retain 90% of America's wealth leaving only ten percent of our money in all forms in the hands of the reminder of 70 million families who do not enjoy status through such contacts or groups ,they work for a living or are underemployed.or have no jobs at all.

The corporately controlled Supreme Court Catholic five recently decided a case that allows industry and it's captains to donate uncontrolled sums of money to their causes during and before elections. STRAW MAN PACS. Further - candidates such as Rick Scott, the Medicare fraudster who paid more than 70 million of his own "fortune" to buy his own Florida governor's candidacy and Donald Trump who bragged he had 600 million of his own money to run for President of the United States , are just two examples showing the power of the uncontrolled dollar in American political life.

People with this wealth can control millions of other people just by the strength of the lies they tell and how they tell them during a campaign. Ask how a man who headed up a healthcare firm,HCA that paid a billion, 700 million dollars in fines for fraud to Medicare in a state like Florida so dependent on that institution can become governor and win chief executive control of the state in a free election unless the voters are totally American idiots ? Please answer me by letter. One FL acquaintance of mine voted for him because Scott stated he would increase jobs which after 30 months has not happened. Really, honest? No single man in a US governorship creates jobs ,the power to do so comes from the nation's capitol ,Wall Street et al and from national commerce and from economic conditions abroad.

What Scott is doing is stripping Florida's 90% of benefits needed to stay alive or educate their families as those suckers born every minute in the"SunshineState"suffer badly and cause his polls to plummet below 35%.

And yet idiotically a local newspaper, Limbaugh on steroids, and rallies for Republicans in the smugly self satisfied community of 50,000 retirees THE VILLAGES show strong , even rabid support to Republicans and their tax cut promises by three delusional presidential candidates. Talk about Kool Aid? All restaurants in the area offer substantial half price drinks, some all day. No wonder.

Returning to the current worldwide depression, and it really is one, the result of the unequal dispersion of monies has caused governments worldwide to force feed funds into economies to keep worldwide economies working at a liveable or at least survival level. And while the United States has contracted a desperate fiscal illness lingering on the brink saved only because of Trillions of borrowed funds started by Bush/Paulson ,continued by Obama/Geithner and post-poned payback by more than fifty years. In this globalization the rest of the world is desperately ill but is being kept alive by financial manipulators in various G 7 nation working their own Black magic or as George Bush Sr.called it,VOODOO Economics.Whatever works is needed,Voodoo or not.

We do know the Laffer curve makes the world laff.!

Economic Sickness in Greece,(which only represents less than 1/4% of world trade0 ,Spain and other parts of EuropE and slowing growth in China is hurting American recovery which had begun in the year of 2012.Now,we are not sure?

OBAMA -LOWEST PAID US PRESIDENT FACING THE GOP OBSTRUCTION FILIBUSTERS.

In 2011 THE CEO of a power company was paid 110 times as much money in one year as the president of the United States of America no doubt according to terms of an employment contract .Could this man possibly have contributed to his single company more value than the leader of the "free world" does in a year to the entire world?

And do ball players who "work" for the Yankees baseball team really EARN 10, 20 and 30 times more than the leader of the United States of America Because they contribute more to mankind and the world? The problem of compensation is coming up more and more in the news and will eventually have to be regulated by a cap by industry and the government in some fashion because it has contributed to the downfall of America in many ways in the past half century. Somehow,someday?

Since I was invested in the stock Reebok I researched payment to the president of the sneaker company perhaps 15-18 years ago. He contractually bargained for payment on the "gross receipts" of the company after having transferred manufacturing to the far east. Reebok was able to price goods low enough to enlarge sales massively so his pay exceeded $25 million dollars for one year, his salary was less than one million but what a bonus. And this contract lasted for ten years and was agreed to by the board of directors.

So as President Obama wakes each morning FACING THE PROBLEMS of AMERICA and the world does he ever reflect on the pay that other luminaries in the spotlight earn for doing far less with NO bearing on the good of the world, and the future of the planet?

He could compare his gross pay about $760,000. per year with the income of his soon to be competitor for the Whitehouse in the 2012 election amounting last year to in excess of 21 million dollars of "retirement" pay, much of it" unearned". Taxed low at 14%. Such a deal !

Barack Obama's critics from the fairly unbalanced network, Fox "News" recently were awarded contracts on income from their broadcast appearances of TEN MILLION DOLLARS per year and that is for being critical or even lying about the president at times. As they choose. They've been at it since 1996.

In the world of Basketball ,a favorite Sport and relaxation of President Obama people like the star of Dallas Mavericks Dirk Nowitzki earn NINETEEN MILLION DOLLARS per year, THERE ARE OTHERS WITH EQUALLY EXORBITANT SALARIES. Average in the league is FIVE.1 MILLION FOR JOURNEYMEN PLAYERS.TOP EARNERS ARE:

PLAYERS	TEAMS	2011 / 2012 SALARIES
1. Kobe Bryant	Los Angeles Lakers	$25.2 million
2. Rashard Lewis	Washington Wizards	$22.1 million
3. Tim Duncan	San Antonio Spurs	$21.3 million
4. Kevin Garnett	Boston Celtics	$21.2 million
5. Gilbert Arenas	Orlando Magic	$19.2 million
6. Dirk Nowitzki	Dallas Mavericks	$19.0 million
7. Paul Gasol	Los Angeles Lakers	$18.7 million
8. Carmelo Anthony	New York Knicks	$18.5 million
9. Amare Stoudemire	New York Knicks	$18.2 million
10. Joe Johnson	Atlanta Hawks	$18.0 million
11. Dwight Howard	Orlando Magic	$17.8 million
12. Elton Brand	Philadelphia 76ers	$17.0 million
13. Deron Williams	New Jersey Nets	$16.3 million
14. Chris Paul	New Orleans Hornets	$16.3 million
15. LeBron James	Miami Heat	$16.0 million
16. Chris Bosh	Miami Heat	$16.0 million
17. Dwyane Wade	Miami Heat	$15.5 million
18. Paul Pierce	Boston Celtics	$15.3 million
19. Andrew Bynum	Los Angeles Lakers	$15.1 million
20. Antawn Jamison	Cleveland Cavaliers	$15.0 million
21. Rudy Gay	Memphis Grizzlies	$15.0 million
22. Brandon Roy	Portland Trailblazers	$14.9 million

| 23. Chauncey Billups | New York Knicks | $14.2 million |
| 24. Al Jefferson | Utah Jazz | $14.0 million |

And that's just Basketball,there are thousands of glaring examples of our shallow judgment and immature values in many other sports and the entertainment industry. Wall Street and industry also excel in excessive rewards of executives compared to elected leaders . A billion a year - not uncommon.

Responsibility for national and international well being and safety scarcely equals the economic reward of unimportant skills or manipulation of numbers or markets, institutions like banks,funds and commodities. This Longstanding Structure of imbalance in Fiscal Reward in the richest country in the world demonstrates to others on the planet America's lack of appreciation, values and priorities.. ,we are the dumbest of all " civilized" societies on the face of the earth because we put ourselves in the position of having the most to lose. We should be ashamed but we're not . NOPE.

Two terms of the American presidency, 8 years earns what the average NBA player GETS IN 8 MONTHS. And players in every sport can reap millions in endorsements for T shirts ,balls, sneakers, etc.

Considering Obama is not greedy as some politicians in the past why does he bother ? Maybe someone will pass the hat and buy him a home on the Pacific palisades TAX FREE upon retirement .Perhaps the socialists if there are any?

Urgent Heartfelt Letter to Ex Ambassador Jon M. Huntsman Posted to2known addresses,never replied.

May 27, 2011

Dear Ambassador Huntsman

It's hard to believe that any sensible caring and PATRIOTIC American would want to run for President on the Republican ticket after what a fifty year collection of self seeking dishonest people has done to America in the last half century.

Senator Ensign,(be kind to your office staff) John Kyl ,the Time magazine compromiser of truth (liar@90%) Congressperson Bachmann (no further comment needed) and Newt Gingrich of the patriotic sex drive stand out as examples of the ignorant duplicity, immorality and greed typified by a Republican standard bearer. Need I mention Sarah ?

Florida Governor Rick Scott of the ill gotten gains,record fines and bought with dirty money election stands out as well. There are more but why bother? New Presidential candidates will associate themselves with this low life group and of necessity assimilate their characteristics. GOP has come to mean the Gas and Oil Party or Guns on Parade indicating that many Americans know where the party derives its' obscene corporate financial support. And the corporate lackeys on the Supreme Court reinforce same.

Forgetting for the moment the current tragedy of a bankrupt nation with two ten year losing wars as a Bush legacy - looking further back we see the first American president in history who felt he had to deny being a "crook" after having preserved the evidence that he most certainly was in his own government archives. And then before resigning he appointed his closest henchman the amenable affable Vice President Ford to the role of President, the only quick fix that could in turn pardon him and preserve his so called legacy and save his glowering face. So transparent and disgusting and yet they survived.

These despicable figures falsely claim they are conservative when in fifty years there has never been a Republican administration that balanced the federal budget and in fact the party's hero of the century Reagan tripled the deficit in his eight non war-time years in office and sometimes accepted his wife's advice on policy based on horoscopes . He also accepted a tax free mansion on the Pacific Ocean.

His associates covered up his Alzheimers evident while in office though his own son now readily admits the affliction What a group! And they promote Republican disastrous economic views that have been forced on the populace through politically dishonest methods backed by billions of dollars from self dealing corporations that have seen to it that personal and corporate taxes that accumulate 90% of income in the top ten percent of the greedy who support them leaving nothing for the fast expiring middle class who must work and spend to keep the economy going, the failure of which is now painfully apparent for middle class citizens and America. Please do not add to this misery, you are too honest to be a Republican of current mold

Sincerely, Jack Doyle

AMERICAN TERRORISTS- THE NRA

Americans should hope and pray that Congressman Peter King after he insulates America from dangerous Muslim extremists will take on the real terrorist organization within our borders.

United States made guns are being smuggled to Mexican drug cartels at an estimated rate of10,000 per week. Furthermore every day guns from Florida and other states that think guns shows requiring no registration are fun are smuggled to States that have sensible laws about concealed weapons. Ask residents of Newark, and Camden, Brooklyn and Philadelphia ,KC and LA . It goes on. American children, housewives , pizza guys ,and police die from these mobile profit driven guns.

Despite the efforts of America's military forces at the bankrupting cost of trillions of dollars spread out over the past sixty years in Korea, Vietnam, Iraq, Afghanistan - we are not "safe" even in our own shoes as we go about our daily lives due to the efforts of a homegrown corporate terrorism sponsor, the NRA.

Ask residents of Newark Camden,Paterson,etc.in New Jersey. And of course Brooklyn ,LIC and NYC,Chicago,KC,LA, etc.

Owning a gun is no security factor, ask ex Congresswoman Gifford of Arizona who" owns a Glock "and knows how to use it. Will she be able to use a bullet damaged brain to pass safe gun laws in the future? Not really, she has retired for the time being due to health problems from a serious head wound by another Arizona "Glock" owner. You can carry a gun around anywhere in AZ, makes ya safe?

There is a gun for every adult in the country most of them able to snuff out an innocent life before any action can be taken by police or citizenry to prevent that finality. 258 million guns. Every year just over 30,000 people die in the US from gunshot wounds. Every two years more US citizens are killed by guns than during all of the Vietnam war.

And it is done for profit with the permission of our "government" indeed even encouraged by many elected officials. Our own liberal President is tongue tied....maybe in a second term?

Political efforts by the National Rifle Association are giving immense financial support to Senators and Congressmen who have encouraged soft laws on death dealing weapons of all description. Most sections of our country have soft or no restrictive "carry "laws protecting unsuspecting Americans from death by deliberate or accidental discharge of weapons. The term RIFLE in the name of this organization is a misleading fiction as more and more dollar volume and profit leads away from hunting deer rifles and shotguns supplanted by carbines and fast action high capacity automatic handguns such as the GLOCK designed for killing human beings .

Weak gun laws enable our arms industry to smuggle to Mexico arming drug cartels there who in turn smuggle workers, sex slaves, drugs and purse snatchers to decimate the United States in various ongoing ways leaving dead victims and poverty stricken shadow illegals in their wake. They dilute jobs, healthcare and education.

This at a cost of billions to the citizens of "the land of lost opportunity", good old suckerland USA. And a lotta dead population.

Congressman Peter King should be strenuously be investigating the organization that terrorizes Congress ,The National "Rifle" Association. Muslims that plot to invade Fort Dix or cut down the Brooklyn Bridge with a power saw in broad daylight, or drive across the Canadian border with dynamite openly in the trunk of a car do not concern me.

Nor are my grandchildren being indoctrinated into a religion that requires dropping everything ,bending down to pray 8 times a day on a rug they must carry. (No city or town in the United States is aiming to install Sharia law to legislate Americans. Aside to Candidate Newt) Honestly Mr. Gingrich,look around you. But you and King should check on the harm the NRA is doing, visit the victims!

SUGGESTION BY REPUBLICAN PUNDITS; Balance Budget on Social Security Ponzi Rework

When I first started working as a Jr. Executive for a corporation I thought I knew about FICA and how the funds were put aside in small amounts, matched by my employer and when I reached the age of 65 there would be a small nest egg type pension for me to retire on. I had no idea what they were invested in but in my dreamily ignorant world felt surely in bank stocks, bonds or savings accounts.

At that time the amount was only about 2% of my salary or less That would have been 1957 or thereabouts and the subject never crossed my mind as to how important this program would be for me and future generations as time went by.

It came to me years later when I was listening to a radio political/economics show that the FICA deductions were being invested in Treasury bills and as the bills matured during the Reagan years and prior the proceeds were spent on Atomic Armaments and aircraft carriers.

We had on hand over 70,000 atomic bombs and of course many aircraft carriers, I visited a few. America the powerful had enough atomic power to destroy the world and it's military nations 1000 times over, military experts estimated that "only 80"A bombs would destroy Russian nuclear capabilities and since they would retaliate with at least 40 or more both countries would be smoldering in devastated unlivable radioactive toxic ruins for decades to come. The estimate regarding the cost of this useless arsenal that only now in 2011 is being reduced in large percentages is 12 Trillion dollars in today's'money (long spent)but this asinine military potlatch has already wreaked havoc on our economy (70 Trillion dollar deficit) and will for centuries.

Chairman Paul Ryan , UP YOURS.

Now it is doubtful that I was the only American working stiff that was hoodwinked into thinking he was safe along with his money .Probably 80% of us suckers were.

By the same token how many Americans knew about our wasteful arsenal of unusable A bombs?

But"conservative"s have now reached the bottom of the funding barrel and their"experts"want us to reconfigure Social Security to pay for past horrific Military Industrialist profits,, Tax cuts for Millionaires dating back to Reagan? there will be no"clawing back" of profits in the trillions over decades or taxes not levied,---SS recipients must skip the dentist, forget the grandkids birthdays and graduation presents or any life enhancing things they need, it is time for austerity by the ancients since they are old ,useless and suckered ,duped by their past" freely elected rulers".

Reform by these "experts"such as Paul Ryan now head of the Congressional Tax Committee, a suddenly important Congressman from Wisconsin,the union busting state (who postulates as a specialist, Include CORPORATE TAX CUTS PLUS ENABLING TEMPORARY BUSH TAX CUTS " PERMANENT FOREVER.!!! Sounds GREAT if your are the wealthy owner of a corporation, right? Oh ,yeah, tack on a national sales tax (8%) that will prevail most heavily on the middleclass and make up for the taxes NOT LEVIED ON CORPORATIONS AND THE WEALTHY. That's Republican "equity".

Mr. Ryan was at one point mentored by Jack Kemp the ex Buffalo football player -Congressman whose ideas in the Congress and as a candidate for President never gained traction because they stunk then and now. Must have been KEMP'S undiagnosed concussions.

Ryan has mastered being a political chameleon first championing the multibillion dollar Wall Street Bail out on the Congress floor,INCLUDING TARP RELIEF and then joining with the Teaparty to condemn overspending- urging fiscal restraint suddenly eureka, DISCOVERED.! .Obviously his Wall Street support is strong. And oh yes ,he was one of the first of three GOP"YOUNG GUNS" in Congress. Rah Rah ..... Reminiscent of the HITLER YOUTH. And he works out, so manly and handsome! And Nazi !

This guy should frighten us all because an analysis of his plans shows his claims in a" planned-road map for the future" reveals it is similar to Reagan Voodoo economics ,gradually reducing Medicare and Medicaid to rag doll status for beneficiaries while increasing the deficit several trillion dollars over the term of his plan which we should hope will never see the light of legislative reality. Medicare will be run by insurance companies and the government will supposedly send a block grant to each state to be divided among those who need healthcare.. you as a member of Us Suckers will buy a plan from the insurance companies as they are presented. Good luck.

Federal Money sent to the States now to help homeowners get relief from foreclosure is now being secretly diverted to many other purposes to balance the mostly Republican shortfalls because Statehouses will not increase taxes on corporations or citizens making a million dollars per year!

Your average elderly person's income is $19,000.The union busting governor of Wisconsin Mr. Scott, and his clowns will parcel it out? How large an allowance will take care of your medical needs and will it be granted by people like the other Governor Rick Scott of Florida?.(The pill mill lover of Medicare scams).

Look up the critique of the openly disastrous Ryan plan written by Paul Krugman, nobel prize winning economist who is very critical and note that Krugman is not running for office .Perhaps we should have had President Reagan's economic plans analyzed years ago by other than paid eye shaded hacks.

The United States is drawing near a point where intelligent discourse has become impossible because of the clamor of 94 rabble elected in the last Congressional election, a tragedy that has happened due to the support of Fox news and cleverly laid plans to sell the cult like group to the Sheeple who watch that network of orchestrated pro GOP liars.

The Best defense is a good offense was never truer than in the context of warfare.. It is essential to understand the essence of the Muslim extremist thrust which is to either convert all those people who do not believe as they do or failing conversion to kill them. This explains their desire to totally destroy Israel and the Jewish religion.

Unfortunately America has chosen to believe in the Christian doctrine of forgiving and turning the other cheek, bargaining and cajoling, threatening, boycotting and a host of other ineffectual actions when confronted with foreign intrusions of any sort.

Let's contemplate what it cost us to allow a group of " religious students" to seize our embassy in Iran back in Carter's single term as an ineffectual intelligent president.

Also what it has cost us to allow Afghanistan to harbor Bin Laden after 9/11 and our reliance on the movement of forces from here in The United States to a country with no roads or government to remove the Taliban from power (if only for a short time.) and the ensuing debacle of the insurgency of bearded sandeled tribesmen armed with Uzis and IED's

In the first case Jimmy Carter decided to try without success to rescue the embassy staff with inappropriate equipment and a heroic doomed Captain America effort. He completely ignored the internationally known fact that when an embassy is taken over by another nation that is an act of WAR If the offended nation does not declare war on the other that is the start of a massive defeat on the international scene de facto.

OPEC be damned, they needed us as customers and in a score of other ways and the dropping of appropriately reduced power Atomic bombs in Iran would have held off any thought by later Muslim extremist s(including Bin laden) of attacks on the United States in any form for fear of total retaliatory destruction.

The same holds true in the case of Afghanistan.

A well placed atomic weapon in the area of Bin Laden's group in Afghanistan would have prevented the following;

Our invasion of Iraq at a cost of thousands of American lives, the earned enmity and contempt of one and a half billion Muslims who now have no fear of us and the resulting complete bankruptcy of our capitalistic banking system.

The loss of our wars in Iraq and Afghanistan. *

The collapse of the world economy because we undertook more than any nation could afford under the leadership of a neuter completely unsuited for his position..

The plan of Bin Laden was clear and is more obvious today .He can justifiably feel he has won a jihad against the United States.

Please recall when the Communist Manifesto by

Karl Marx stated"We will force the capitalist nations to spend themselves into destruction "

Bin Laden adopted this same concept (SIC) "When we send out two warriors to unfurl a banner showing Al Quaida you Americans spend 100 million dollars dispatching 10,000 Marines to that area something we will force you to do time and again until you have exhausted your wealth."

So read the newspapers, look at the TV and Google the internet and learn how this has become a reality.

*As of March 2009 we are sending 17,000 more troops to Afghanistan and probably more later. Our Generals state flatly we have not won the war and in Iraq we still have over 300,000 Americans in harms way ,truck drivers and "Diplomat Guards " costing upwards to $400,000 each per year and news article dumbly point out that insurgent attacks have "diminished" to 100 per week.Oh, only a hundred?

As of March . 2009 -Casualties - 240 dead Iraqis per month and a few dozen American soldiers And this is an "improvement" ? NOTE; Thousands of tribal Insurgents (sunnis) have been paid to stop killing American or coalition forces and at this writing Iraq is taking over the cost of making these payments with a dwindling budget because of the drop in oil prices.

There are upwards to 100,000 recipients of these bribes set up by Gen Petreaus

You may well ask what would have happened if we had employed Atomic Weaponry in the middle east so please observe how the Japanese occupations by the Allied US forces went and how our relations with the now peaceful country have gone since Hiroshima and Nagasaki.

This writer was an occupation troop in German after WW 2 and lived with the Germans and other American troops with wives off post in an apartment built from the rubble of bombed out ruins.. There was no insurgence because defeat was self evident and we had the Marshall plan which helped Europe including Germany rebuild under intelligent supervision and their own plans. Businesses thrived and American were welcome and"liked"

Now compare!

COMING SOON IN A FAILING GOVERNMENT TOO NEAR YOU !

"Noogie" (My nickname) Nuttwist Norquist, the anti tax demon has struck again entering the United States Congress's argument about the 2012 never to be passed budget. This pudgy effete snob pimping for Americans For Tax Reform is a perfect example of what comes from the spoiled wealthy upbringing of a person who never had to shovel snow ,dig a ditch or cut the grass. He is currently middle aged, paid by wealthy coporations and persons to attack and destroy elected officials seeking to pass a Federal tax in any fashion because he feels, in addition to being well compensated for it, this is anathema to good governing. Congressmen in particular cow down to the non enforcea- ble pledge they signed at his urging to garner favor ,brown nose points with" Conservatives" and their voting records who have flopped together like cow dung in a barn during a subzero winter in Montana. Hence- brownnose.

It really is not NN (though he really is detestable) I am offended by but the elected officials in Congress who took an oath of office that certainly overrides any oath to plump Noogie. Their job is to keep government financed with a prospect of a tomorrow for the present and future gener- ations with no shutdowns or credit downgrades from the world markets ,which is also in terrible fiscal status..

FURTHER; The election of the Teaparty Republicans if you can call them that,has presented America and the House of Reprehensibles with phantasizers who believe there is no consequence for American default and or standstill . At least some of them feel that way and House majority ``leader '' Boehner and weasel Cantor cannot or will not control them at the most inopportune times.Another "doomsday" is approaching at the end of Dec. or Jan. 1,2013.

The best hope is there will be a groundswell of votes against a substantial percentage of these non operative amateurs at governance so that there is hope AT THE START OF next year of a budget that does not condemn millions of downtrodden middle lower class people to sickness and even death while replenishing funds dedicated to the ranks of teachers, construction workers, police , firemen and research techs infrastructure and salaries. A GREAT CHANGEOVER MUST be made and the next election is in poker terms the ''ALL IN" EFFORT, HOUSE ,SENATE AND PRESIDENCY. MAKE NO MISTAKE !

JACK DOYLE Wrote: (your comment) RE; Universal Healthcare

Such baloney IN THE Wall Street Journal article !"Unlimited Federal Power" -as in when they can draft your 18 year old kid and send him to fight in Vietnam or Korea where nobody in America has ever been or seen on a map but he is told he is fighting to "protect American freedom" .And we lose?Tens of thousands of men and Billions of Dollars?

Or when a man joins the National guard and finds the government has defined NATIONAL interest as far as Iraq 7000 miles away and four tours of duty while your family loses the house and lives on relatives,charity and food stamps for years .And you come home with no legs? Or in a body bag? And we lose?

And every state in America Republican or Democrat REQUIRES you to buy Auto insurance to drive A CAR.That's Commerce by any definition.

WHY IS IT TAKING FREEDOM AWAY when we ask a citizen to share the cost of HIS OWN MEDICAL CARE THROUGHOUT

LIFE when every other industrialized nation has such a plan? That's commerce.

When you are born you need a Doctor, Nurse and Hospital-some one must pay for those services,.a SERIOUSACCIDENT along the highway and in life you may require hundreds of THOUSANDS OF DOLLARS IN IMMEDIATE MEDICAL CARE! .So you must pay for it .Does the citizen ,have $150,000 in his wallet ? As you lay Bleeding should yhour neighbors let you lie on the curb and die?

Those are your PRECEDENTS $SUPREMES call your corporate sponsors and your wives and ask them what to do! And pass the bill as legal which it is. How is your medical insurance and who pays for it?

LEND LEASE A BETTER DEAL THAN FLAT EARTH

At the end of WW2 we had the very bright idea of helping the struggling conquered and previously occupied nations of Nazi German to get to their feet and start self supporting their countries in industry and commerce by seeding them with American wealth even though we were deeply in debt ourselves nationally.

The details are at this point in my story - not important -but IT WORKED.

At one time this writer was critical of Japan and the aid they received from us because they became a more powerful nation than we could afford. I thought so then and man, was I right.

Any viewing of imported automobile statistics will reveal how much our adminstration's generous allowances to them cost Detroit, the UAW and American economy during A 40 year period after the second world war were a harbinger of the mess we now find ourselves in.

What was "good for General Motors is good for the nation and visa versa" said Sec. Of Defense Charles Wilson during the Eisenhower administration and truer words were never spoken. True GM was forced by the strength of the union into too generous contracts to the benefit of it's workers. However those retail establishments that depended on them and our nation's economy thrived during that period with low unemployment, higher than usual GDP and nearly balanced budgets in Washington DC. Ike's administration while boring was in my opinion honest and true in devotion to the overall American population and benefited no particular interest groups.-

.One year of eight the national budget was balanced while Ike was in office .

That was the ONLY REPUBLICAN PRESIDENTIAL BALANCED BUDGET IN OVER 70 YEARS.! I know because I lived throughout this period

.Hard to believe,? As Casey Stengel said"You could look it up".

Then came the Reagan years when Japanese electronics and Auto imports were taking over 20 percent of our volume in those areas. Car quotas were relaxed from Japan and the quality products flooded in because the factories were copying the good features of American know how and incorporating REFINED features mechanically and electronically.

As thanks for these relaxed standards Reagan was paid by a group in Japan one million dollars for a speech that lasted one hour after which he fell asleep at the the table .He had already left the office of President and was no doubt showing his alzheimers whatever stage.

To return to my point however if one took the "flat earth" figures, statistics will show that American exports have never come close to the costs of overseas job losses in trade pacts , fast track deals that screwed so many American Union and non union workers promising 55 year olds new job training. This for people who had run machines that made metal parts , underwear, socks and T shirts prepping them for technical skills (that if absorbed at all).where for the most part geographically there were no local industries that could use their newly found abilities in the Carolinas, Tennessee, Alabama and many other sparsely populated southern states .

Statistically if we were to take the dollar costs of the unemployment , early retirement, and welfare by State ,County and Municipality, the cost to American industry as a whole (not to mention alcoholism ,mental illness and health costs of unemployed and underemployed of this group) we would find "globalism" to be a rather FULL CROCK THAT IS OVERFLOWING with lies and excrement from Washington DC scriptwriters.

And of course there were the"wars", none won except for Bosnia,thanks Bill Clinton.

And we never submitted an invoice except for the First Gulf War. And we lost that one since we had to fight it all over again starting in 2002 because of "TheBig Lie",

'WEAPONS OF MASS DECEPTION" WRITTEN BY BUSH/CHENEY AND Co- produced BY FOX NEWS NETWORK. And co-participated in by the American News media asleep all the while. (Even they know it)

Military Misadventures of the past 60 years The Wasted Wars and Fortunes

Korea	One Trillion dollars 54,000 US troops killed,102,000 wounded
Vietnam	584 Billion dollars 58,000
Lebanon	100 Milllion one month invasion- 258 a tragedy of policy!
Mogadishu	"BlackHawk Down" see the movie another tragedy of US humiliation
Iraq	See Later Section of this book we all are living it still- encouraged by *MIC
Afghanistan	Afgoinonagain, forever encouraged by red blooded Republicans and MIC

*MILITARY INDUSTRIALIST COMPLEX Ike warned future Americans about, championed by Reagan.

Despite the marshaled efforts of America's armed forces at the cost of trillions of dollars spread over the past sixty years we are not "safe"even in our own shoes as we go about our daily lives due to the efforts of a homegrown corporate terrorism sponsor, the NRA. Most recently three teenage high school students in Ohio were shot dead before10 A.M. in their cafeteria by a classmate with a legal 22 caliber automatic handgun.

There is a gun for every adult in the country most of them able to snuff out an innocent life before any action can be taken by police or citizenry to prevent that finality. 258 million guns.The number is the one we know about.

And it is done for profit with the permission of our "government"indeed even encouraged by many elected officials. This fact is now either ignored or approved by most of the population of the United States.

Election efforts by the politically entrenched National Rifle Association give immense financial support to Senators, Congressmen and local officials who have encouraged soft laws on death dealing weapons of all description. Most sections of our country have soft or no restrictive"carry"laws protecting unsuspecting Americans from death by deliberate or accidental discharge of weapons. Meanwhile Police groups all over the United States call for control of firearms and they are ignored, also shot dead at times.

The term RIFLE in the name of this organization is misleading as more and more dollar volume and profit leads away from hunting "long guns" to carbines and fast action high capacity automatics such as the GLOCK designed for killing human beings. A majority of hunters of game in America are not members of the NRA. Ask Congresswoman Gabby Gifford of AZ. whose life and future has been ruined by permissive gun laws that are totally outlandishly death defying ridiculous in the wild west state she represented.(past tense)

See my letter to her in this book.

Congressman Peter King 339 Cannon House Office Building Washington, D.C. 20515

March 7, 2011

Dear Sir,

You talk about terrorists ,my grand kids have not had any lessons in school about Muslims or Sharia and there is no chance of it happening. Most Muslim terrorists have been exceedingly dumb and quickly apprehended. Such as the one who was cutting down the Brooklyn bridge in broad daylight with a powersaw.

9/11 was the exception because we were stupid enough to leave cockpit doors wide open on all airlines.

However despite the marshaled efforts of America's military forces at the cost of trillions of dollars and thousands of lives spread out over the past sixty years we are not "safe"even in our own shoes as we go about our daily lives due to the efforts of a homegrown corporate terrorism sponsor, the NRA. Ask Gabby about it.(You know, the attractive intelligent Representative from Arizona with a Glock)

As you must know there is a gun for every adult in the country most of them able to snuff out an innocent life before any action can be taken by police or citizenry to prevent that finality. (258 million guns. (Every year just over 30,000 people die in the US from gunshot wounds. Every two years more US citizens are killed by guns than in all of the Vietnam war.)

And it is done for profit with the permission of our "government" indeed even encouraged by many elected officials, probably including you. This fact is now ignored or approved by most of the population of the United States.

Political efforts by the National Rifle Association are giving immense financial support to Senators and Congressmen who have encouraged soft laws on war making weapons of all description. Most sections of our country have soft or no restrictive"carry"laws protecting unsuspecting Americans from death by deliberate or accidental discharge of weapons. The term RIFLE in the name of this organization is a misleading fiction as more and more dollar volume and profit leads away from hunting "longguns' to carbines and fast action high capacity automatic handguns such as the GLOCK designed for killing human beings .

Weak gun laws enable our arms industry in smuggling 10,000 guns per week to Mexico to arm drug cartels there who in turn smuggle sex slaves,drugs and job snatchers to decimate the United States in various ongoing ways leaving dead victims and poverty stricken shadow Mexican illegals in their wake.

This at a cost of billions to the citizens of "the land of opportunity" ,good ol suckerland.

How about jumping on the NRA? After all they are already terrorizing Congress.

Sincerely,

Jack Doyle

Previously we touched on the Socialist Party but in the United States the referral seems to evoke symbols of anarchy, explosions, Eugene V. Debs and other negative things that make folks here in America, the "home of democracy" evoking explosive horrific scenes.

Nothing could be further from the actual facts of the socialist theory and practice..

Norway is a case in point which in 2008 had a surplus, no debt and a living standard far in excess of the United States. They have an opera house in Oslo that cost 800 million dollars, we have an over budget embassy in Bagdead that cost an estimated(still adding up) 600 million dollars that will take over 1500 people to staff , probably thousands more armed troops to protect it from suicide bombings for as long the the place serves as an American embassy.. Since it is in the "Green Zone is is not easy to reach for the average bear or Iraqi or American tourist if and when they go there which could be decades.

Naturally it can be pointed out that Norway as is the case with every Socialist country has never taken on the role of world "cop" to prevent a host of evil "Isms"such as Facism,Communism, Muslim Theocracy,(i.e the Taliban) from spreading worldwide.

As a result we are in debt and they enjoy the famous 4 fruits of freedom from Wars that we fought or are now fighting.

In the main the United Nations was to spread the cost of "policing" " but only in the first Gulf War did the cost of a necessary war get divvied up among countries who benefited from stopping Hussein's Iraq from conquering large portions of the oil countries and putting them under one dictatorship..This is to the first Bush's credit.

The next disastrous war against Iraq still has paid under the table Republican supporters writing books and articles and making Sunday talk show appearance pointing out how necessary it was to stop the snake before it left the garden known as the "Bush Doctine".

Iraq was a Neocon hoax wimpishly agreed to by Congress's both parties.

The logic of a preemptive strike is weak as a kitten-. North Korea for instance –devising an Atomic bomb .Go back to other eras, China ,Russia and over 7 dictatorships in South America flourished as the US looked on even as we spent billions on "Defense".

The facts are we have never been able to remotely afford the nationalistic war like efforts we have made by any stretch of the imagination which has put America in the 64 Trillion dollar debt dungeon that exists in the year 2009. We borrowed from communists to do this!

Some of the Billions should have been put into Mexican border defense with armed troops and fences just like Israel has now and East Germany had during the cold war.

This would have protected us from the flood of illegals gaining a foothold here by having babies who became automatic Americans while parents were criminally in our nation.

Preventive expense against illegal drugs ,people smuggling and the like would have born fruit in many ways since we do not know how many border crossers were Al Quada in disguise waiting to form groups with hand grenades ,rocket launchers and roadside or mall bombs waiting for a grand stand large scale attack on the civilian population or worse yet on schoolyards across the nation in one horrible scene of mass murder and destruction.

Perhaps on a Christmas eve or on Labor Day .how nasty ! Implausible, maybe ! Morale damaging ,oh, most certainly.

We have put up with this silent invasion for decades and every adminstration puts the dangers and future conse- quences in it's deepest pocket and buries it in palaver of some sort,-----

And someday it may come to roost like exploding subway cars in London.

THE NEW REPUBLICAN ROTPACK

If there is any way the Gas and Oil party can show disdain for the American people they find it. Within Congress they are packing proposals one after the other with ways to harm laws already on the books or to invent new ones that harm the environment and places where"real" Americans live or vacation.

Right now they are busy doing the bidding of corporations that support them with campaign donations trying to pre- vent any governmental restrictions on removing mountain- tops to dig for coal leaving debris in streams and lakes that should be left alone because they lead to drinking water aquifers and opening new digging for minerals near the Grand Canyon National Park vacation locations and a host of other anti Environmental actions at the demands of coal and oil barons.

The Rotpack is also busily interfering with and interjecting problems for the Consumer Protection Agency which was developed by the Obama administration as a remedy for years of ongoing and constant illegal machinations of agencies dealing with banking ,insurance, investment and real estate cheating consumers in all ways they could devise with subtle or obvious government involvement.

The Republicans in the Whorehouse of Reprehensible have flat out refused to agree to any presidential appointment to head the agency. They, including Congressman Issa (as in ISSA t an honest man?) insist on a managing committee which famously is a horse that developed by competing views into an ugly camel designed to be a flatulent muck maker. They do not appear to be on the side of the American consumer but on the side confidence men who will surely appear if laws that benefit regular Americans who seek loans.insurance,homes and safe honest investments are circumvented and avoided entirely even before they are proposed.

Congressman Issa is the wealthiest man in Congress with a net worth of over 250 Million dollars and has an INTERESTING previous criminal record including car theft, he was under investigation for arson as well.,he now looks for criminality and wrong doing as head of the Congressional oversight committee. Perhaps that was an oversight ! Suggestion; look him up ,he's clever, underhanded ,ambitious and wealthy !

And then examine the recent Republican treatment of the FAA where funds have been held up in their professed call for small (minded)government. Operating funds for the Agency are stopped resulting in a complete halt in collecting a government tax on tickets, furloughing 4000 employees and losing 200 MILLION IN US TAXES EACH WEEK while airport construction and repair projects are halted. Republicans are fighting the unions desire to organize airport workers. It figures!

Disgusting is too kind a term for this new Rotpack that sings and dances to the tune of those corporations who publicly bribe them. And the Republican Party wants no changes to tax laws that benefit the same companies.,strange? They are NOT on the side of the American consumer but on the side of flimflams who are lining up if laws that benefit regular Americans who seek loans.insurance,homes and safe honest investments are circumvented and avoided entirely even before promulgated. This in their professed call for ``small" (minded) government. Operating funds for the Agency are stopped resulting in a complete halt in ticket taxes totaling 200 million dollars per week in government tax on tickets, furloughing 4000 employees while airport construction and repair projects are halted. See later. THIS IS GOP INACTION ADDING DEFICITS.

So let's see how the 1% lives, they could not keep it secret,

HEADLINE; Presidential candidate Romney tears down 12 million dollar California ocean front mansion. New structure to cost over 16 million with an elevator for his automobiles. His wife with 2 Cadillacs who rides her own thoroughbred horses has been described as out of touch with today's working women because she never had a paying job. Her automobiles also relegate other cars to peasant status as almost all cars have never had an elevator of their own in an oceanfront mansion with a swimming pool.

Republicans mouthpieces fight back stating " stay at home mothers work too" though their cars may relax in air conditioned comfort in the garage while Mrs.Ann rides her horsies. Other working women without millionaire hubbies may get to Starbucks for a Latte break so there!

Headline: Retiring Governor Haley Barbour of Miss. pardons four murderers including Brett Favre's brother and relatives of heavy Barbour political donors.The donors contributed heavily and Barbour is not a lightweight. A tag team of him and Gov.Corpulent Christie Of NJ would decimate most Democratic Governors who average less than 200 lbs. even with Union support.

Barbour was considered for a time by the Republican establishment as a True"conservative" who would be a BETTER(?) CHOICE for the party than Romney or any of the 2012 candidates.He declined to run.

This is the one percent. Are they out of touch?

THESE EXAMPLES ARE THE LAST STRAW, DO YOU FEELTHESE ACTIONS AND THE MEN INVOLVED SHOULD REPRESENT YOU FOR THE NEXT 8 YEARS? ARE THEY IN TOUCH WITH YOU?

In the HALF CENTURY past I was an executive in a small conglomerate in a boring industry in the stationery, art and drafting supply field. We absorbed smaller affiliated related product companies,inserted our larger experienced sales force and discarded their factories and superfluous people and gained profit thereby..One industry leading firm we absorbed had a factory in Pennsylvania .and was directly connected to ours in the past with a similar surname.

When my previous firm (MY DEPARTURE WAS SEVERAL YEARS PRIOR) finalized the purchase over 125 people lost their jobs and the products that had been made in America for nearly a century were set up for manufacture in Mexico and later Asia. Planning for this scheme was devised by snobby American MBA grads (a Sanitorum campaign term). Notably education benefits some Americans but not all. The shutdown was in time for Christmas that year. Doubtful there was a company Christmas party.

This was a Bain Capital operation in miniature, made money for American stockholders and added to unemployment in Pennsylvania while new jobs may have opened in Mexico. Proving the world is flat!

The Senate of the United States has shown what Bedlam was all about.

It all starts with the R party that from the outset of the Obama presidency has been looking for every nit pick that can make the Democrats look bad even if only four years from now but most certainly in the midterm elections.

Pardon me if I err in saying the first manure laden brick thrown was the one about "Death Panels" lurking in the medical reform plans of the Democrats who at the outset have sought to cover some 30 to 40 million citizens of our country with health insurance they can afford and to prevent insurance firms from refusing coverage to those who are already ill.

Another canard is the one about rationing healthcare which is what the insurance firms already do but the rabble rousing R's have turned it around in the minds of millions of people with their speeches on the capitol steps, in tea party gatherings in the hustings and in mailings to their so called base. Look up the word base, it has many meanings.

So the Senate has resembled an insane asylum for months now as the healthcare plan is:"debated" with repetition of lies beyond count and even Democrats entering into arguments that have no meaning when the end of medical care for all is considered

.Should a family be forced to give birth to a dead from the outset infant at a cost to themselves and society of hundreds of thousands of dollars? Or even the death of the mother as a result because one elected representative belongs to a certain religion when religion has no function in government according to the constitution of the United States?

The R party will stop at nothing to achieve nothing in government for as long as the Dems are in the majority even if what is being proposed is advantageous to every citizen of the United States of America.

That in a nutshell describes the bedlam we refer to above. As Big Daddy said "MENDACITY". (Cat On a Hot Tin Roof)

And folks like Senator Lieberman are poster Senators for that .He has long been a Repug in Dem clothing and because of circumstances(the need of 60) he still holds power in the Senate as head of a Committee while he deserves a chair that is electrified or a needle that hurts.I was going to say a gas chamber but that would be anti semitic.

CHAPTER 6

THE FUTURE IS NOT CLEAR AND "IT IS NOT OURS TO SEE"

NJ Republican Governor Christie reneged on a bipartisan plan to build a tunnel to NYC from New Jersey.

When even the most unbiased observer takes a calculated guess at the cost of this short sighted decision the future losses in the NJ citizen's ability to be employed in the New York market has to be in the billions of dollars spread over several decades of lost opportunity. Millions have been spent and wasted.

Additional multimillion dollar losses accrue to home values in the NJ area within fifty miles of Manhattan. This because the NJ governor has no interest in adding to future bond issues while there were deficits and obvious debate about current state budgets looming.

The sins of previous Republican president Bush and the massive deficits left, two ongoing wars and the announcement made by Secretary Paulson in October 2008 of impending financial crisis has spread nationwide and worldwide and lies like a fatal fog on every world economy

And in NYC Most dangerous is the possibility of a terrorist attack on the only tunnel connection NJ and NY have. If it is destroyed this can cost us massive destruction to the Metroplitan NY/NJ and American economy, a few guys on the platforms with revolvers are not protection! So again I say, WHY ME?

AND IT'S 101 YEAR OLD! Older than me.

Obamacare & Romneycare Despite protestations THEY ARE THE SAME. Recommended by AARP AND BY ECONOMISTS

Every Day the topics that appear on the internet , TV news and newspapers are the more concerning to the person who understands what is happening and what has occurred in the past 50 years and why.

A case in point is an executive who headed up a health care company and was fined millions of dollars for fraud is now heading up a group that is preaching the dangers of a government inspired health coverage plan with advertisements and broadside TV ads that distort facts… bringing back the Harry and Louise days of the early Clinton administration when the first steps were being taken to bring America kicking and screaming up to par with all the civilized industrial countries in the world in the health care realm.

Since that time when the "Hilary" Clinton National healthcare plan effort was killed by Republicans opposition and advertizing by insurance corporations over 49 Million people have lived without health insurance of any kind and the dolt president bush the second "stated that all Americans have health insurance called the emergency room."

The stupidity of that "let them eat cake" remark can be researched but the simple fact that a person seeking medical care who is in the status of an "emergency" is many times too late, not tended in a preventive manner and may not receive sufficient care to cure the malady they suffer.

Anyone who has sat in a crowded emergency room when not brought in by an ambulance(which is usually an extra $450. cost) can testify to the painful and sometimes aggravating wait that ads to the illness that may turn out to be fatal due to unavoidable delay. EMS is overstressed and so are the emergency room hospital staffs.

Hospitals must defer payments from indigent and low income patients ,those invoices get added to the costs of people who do have medical insurance so that premiums rise for those who do prepare in advance becoming a penalty for preparedness and forward planning.

And the battle for National healthcare for all goes on at this late date 2012,when Germany had it under Bismark during the 1840's, designed to maintain the German workforce members because many of them were emigrating to America for higher wages though without benefits offered by industries.. sound familiar?

And our dear Gas and Oil Party is fighting tooth and nail to prevent healthcare plans from subsidizing women's health issues like birth control dragging in red herrings about religious issues. Such thoughtful people....

And REMEMBER Richard Nixon favored national healthcare in1974 stating from the Whitehouse it would not cost more than the system then in place! He was not all bad, just misguided in his desire TO BE A " WINNER '' like Charley Sheen

UNIVERSAL AMERICAN HEALTHCARE IS HELD UP IN COURT FOR POLITICAL CAUSES,NOT LOGIC OR LEGALLY PREVENTIVE REASONS. PROPOGANDA AGAINST IT IS NOT TO BENEFIT ORDINARY CITIZENS.

CHANGES, THEY SHOULD BE A COMIN'-THE AMERICAN CONSTIPATION !

It would benefit the American system of Justice if we were to stop worshipping an outdated opaque antique icon, the "Constitution of the United States of America."

Sorry flag wavers but it was written over 200 years ago when slavery was legal and admired and there was no instant communication ,, no mass media ,no telephone land line or cell phone, I Pod ,even a ballpoint pen ,frozen food, medical insurance ,automobile,or airplane. It is outmoded ! An Historical LAG HOLDING BACK OUR NATION ,AN ANTIQUE DOCUMENT!

When many of the subjects brought to the United States courts in the 21st Century did not exist adopting a new Constitution now (in the next ten years qualifies) could incorporate new meaning and clarity to current national law that would be meaningful to future centuries and longer.

The Chief Justice of the United States Supreme Court points to the 234 year old anachronism to outlaw a healthcare plan needed by 50 million citizens because the fumbling Fathers did not include the plan in the document. HOW THE HELL COULD THEY ? That's called begging the question as well as an obtuse argument.

Observe how long the 1776 model lasted..To worship and interpret an antique legal document is insane from an ethical and practical standpoint . Another inconvenient truth?

This"worship" is an insane foible of the backward Teaparty and other rigid "conservatives" of self serving convoluted concepts.

The Peeparty stems from the misconception that taxes now levied are similar and as onerous to those complained about in the days before America was a nation. ,Taxation and treasury were located in 2 months distant London, England.

The "Farmers of the Constitution" are best put in the barn and replaced with computer and social media authors using the original as a template for essential direction.....

No founding document 234 YEARS OLD can serve America in the 22nd Century..

The problem is finding Americans who would draw up a new document who would be altruistic, intelligent, forward thinking and have the good of this and future American generations in their *plans. if these people are available please call me, I'm in the book.*

snob champion of NO TAXES EVER,GROVEL NUTTWIST.

I refer of course to Grover Norquist who is paid by the wealthy and super rich to prevent their money from escaping any pursuit that does not profit them.

His theme in TIME is simple,"Could you just leave us alone." Republicans grovel before him because he twists their.... , You know.

Almost all GOP Congressmen and Senators have signed this cult pledge like ALCOHOLICS IN NEED OF SUPPORT.

This guy is president of AMERICANS FOR TAX REFORM and is a lobbyist who covers the waterfront coercing Republican politicians to sign his pledge against raising taxes in turn promising financial support from many self interested greedy groups with secret money for political use against mainly Democrats who have pledged to serve their constituents rather than a blind Daddy Warbucks multi purpose money bank.

When the Democrats or ANY political candidates believe their constituents need a government that requires money for education ,returning soldiers need mental healthcare and paraplegic operations or job training, cities and states need roads and bridges OR the Federal government needs more examiners at the IRS TO APPLY the tax code the Nuttwist pledge should never exist, it is the essence of greedy penurious bastards at the level of governance. And gee, where was it when we invaded Vietnam,Iraq and a numberof other locations without a quote on cost?,

So I will now outline a perfect example of the ONE PERCENT leaving their people alone and SUFFERING TO THE TUNE OF BILLIONS FOR IT. You must recall a man APPOINTED BY GEORGE W. BUSH to chair THE S.E.C. ,one of the one percent born to wealth named Christopher Cox. His Grandfather is deceased President Richard M.Nixon,President of the United States . He married a wealthy heiress and was well educated at Harvard Law and elsewhere, ran for Congress and served Republican Presidents as well as Democrats in appointed posts.

One of Cox's closest friends was Arthur Laffer, whose famous curve drawn on a napkin made him the phoney godfather of supply-side economics. Laffer staunchly defended Cox against conservatives criticizing his inactivity. The chairman, says Laffer, "has got a whole staff there that [has] been appointed by previous people." Well, not exactly. Shortly after Cox took office, The Washington Post reported that senior turnover at the commission gave him "an unusual opportunity" to appoint several key lieutenants. Donaldson had already appointed Linda Thomsen to the second most powerful position at the commission, chief of the Division of Enforcement. Would Cox replace her? No. Thomsen stayed. The decision set the tone for Cox's chairmanship. He would strive to avoid controversy. "In his job, it makes no sense for him to be a bull in a china shop," says Laffer.

My previous feelings about Laffer are further reinforced. It was reported during Cox's tenure investigators who wanted to subpoena documents or compel interviews faced cumbersome processes to gain the commission's approval for each case. Enforcement officials had to see the SEC commissioners (plural)before approaching a company about a civil settlement and Cox personally postponed such cases as Bioval eventually weakening the sanctions sought.

His enforcement against "naked sort selling" was sorely missing according to many former agents interviewed after he was replaced by Susan Shapiro, an Obama appointee.

Allow me now to introduce a Bernie Madoff ,former head of the NASDAQ who" made off "with billions of many other one percenter's lucre in the largest PONZI SCHEME ever perpetrated on the US economy. It started in the 1970s and the collapse due to the costliest whistle ever blown was during Chris Cox's term at the SEC in December of 2008,a period of 38 years. As friend ``W" bush was packing for Texas.

For thirty years Madoff because of his reputation as head of NASDAQ was believed to be a financial genius at profitable trading and was trusted by hundreds of super rich families, among them the owners of the New York Mets baseball team who are even now engaged in litigation involving a loss of over 170 Million dollars they were legally obliged to pay back to other Madoff victims after theWilpons had taken profits from the Ponzi fund.

Numerous whistles blew only excess saliva, one investigation that never happened started at Madoff's firm in Midtown Manhattan and where investigators learned Madoff personally would be their primary contact. He provided them with contradictory information. But when they sought to confront him about it, he said he had already given the information they wanted to investigators in Washington -- which was news to the SEC officials in New York.

Shortly thereafter, they concluded their investigation without answering the questions that had spurred the review. Was this a Cox pre arranged non enforcement pact? Why?

In 2005, fraud analyst and onetime Madoff rival Harry Markopolos wrote a detailed letter to the SEC's Boston office warning, "The world's largest hedge fund is a fraud." The Boston office had worked with Markopolos before and found him credible.

Boston sent the letter to the SEC's New York office, where officials viewed Markopolos skeptically and did not understand his reasoning, which was based largely on statistics. Stats was a tough course in college.The team assigned to look into Madoff had little experience reviewing potential Ponzi schemes.

In May 2006, SEC investigators interviewed Madoff, who didn't bring along a lawyer. When asked how he consistently beat the market, he told the investigators, "Some people feel the market," the report recounts.

Madoff told the inspector general that he expected to be exposed when he told the investigators that his trading was processed through the Depository Trust Co., an important financial intermediary. He gave the SEC his DTC account number, which they could have used to verify the trades he claimed to have made.

"I thought it was the end, game over. Monday morning they'll call DTC, and this will be over," Madoff told the watchdog earlier this year. "And it never happened."

The report calls the agency's decision to never verify Madoff's trading "the most egregious failure in the Enforcement investigation." That investigation was closed in August 2006. It took a single phone call to DTC after the

Ponzi scheme was exposed in December 2008 to find out that he had not placed any trades with his investors' funds.

Concerns about Madoff's firm continued to arrive. In March 2008, the office of then-SEC Chairman Christopher Cox received an e-mail from a source who had contacted the agency several times, urging investigators to look into secret files Madoff maintained on a computer he carried. Cox's aides sent the e-mail to the enforcement division.

An enforcement staffer who had worked on the Madoff case replied: "[W]e will not be pursuing the allegations."

At this point I will make the obvious statement that Madoff after 9 investigations over 30 years was finally found to be a gigantic fraud , hence December 2008 brought down the house of Madoff.! When the stuff hit the fan Cox said in his statement "The commission received"credible and specific allegations regarding Mr.Madoff's financial wrongdoing" but did not respond aggressively ."NO "bull in a china shop-for 50 billion dollars for him! Or Laffable Laffer.

Passing strange, one of the actors on the stage along the way conducting one investigation was Erik Swanson who served as a lawyer for the SEC commission for ten years .He was married to Shanna Madoff in 2007, a niece of Madoff, daughter of his brother Peter who was the firms' compliance officer!

The Dominos and falling cards did not hit her or husband Erik Swanson.

Dominos are so interesting. Surely considering the consequences the"alone" Noogie Nutttwist seeks for himself and his cult at a cost of over 50 Billion dollars and the thousands of ruined lives of investors'families should not be duplicated or sought after by any government official or cloud headed theorist. Or IDIOTIC AMERICAN LOBBYIST.

ALLOW ME TO DIGRESS

As Of Three Days Ago, Rodney King passed away, That was sad because he could have enjoyed the results of his literary pursuits at this stage of life. Surely the beating he took had nothing to do with his death? Ask the LA cops after all the film shows he was still fighting to breath, called resisting arrest..

It has occurred to me to doubt my ability to transform my thoughts into understandable literature or more important—interesting reading and then I recall the chore of reading "Catcher in the Rye" by Salinger and worse yet "the Brother Karamazov" by Dostoyevsky who seemed to forget what he named his characters on previous pages or even chapters. Ol "Dost" seemed to take diabolical pleasure in giving four or five names to the boys in his tome.

And it was so sad and dragging.

As far as the "Catcher" I knew more interesting characters than those drawn in the automobile trips from the thirties depicted in that book and my 1939 Cadillac burning a half quart of oil and 6 gallons of gas per mile would have told more exciting and interesting tales. And don't ask me about Chaucer, Shelley and Keats PUHLEASE.!

And why didn't Shakespeare write in American? These authors were required reading so that's why we all know them! Forced readership I say.

Now I return to the main theme of my literary effort by naming A FEW OF MANY Republicans who sadly are always in the news who are flat out bastards, there are worse terms but I leave it to the NJ Senate president to employ them. As Casey said you"could look it up"

One is Super Gov. Corpulent Christie of NJ who at present is trying to make another attempt at Vice President out of a tax cut in a state that is sliding off a deficit chasm. Vote me in ,I cut taxes is the typical Republican entreaty from desperation gulch in lovely downtown Trenton.(and everywhere)

Governor Christie, serial liar who has publicly been called the sexual appendage (censored) by others ,has cost the people of NJ billions of dollars in a short 18 months in office and has doomed commuters and NYC job seeker to a single underground tube 100 years old for the foreseeable future. All while dropping the ball on a half billion dollars in school aid from the federal govt. and lying about it blaming and firing his educational commissioner, a FORMER FRIEND. The damage to Education in NJ towns is massive and continuing. He has proposed a ten percent income tax cut favoring the richest while the state is broke and owes billions. And the NJ pension fund is 10 years in arrears.His plan to borrow money to finance a deficit is outright SICK considering how broke our grandkids in NJ are already. Christie in his PR efforts refers to the present state of the state as a comeback" by reformers" ,EEEEGH GADS !

Then unfortunately there is Mitch McConnell who truly resembles (take a look) a well dressed turtle.. Mac's major claim to intelligent governing by the minority leader of the US Senate has been to proclaim the "most important thing that we can do is to make Obama a one term president" apparently forgetting the need to replace the many million jobs lost by his party, the need to safely withdraw from the TWO TEN YEAR LOST WARS ,the Trillions in taxes given away to the rich kids and supportive corporations,and a host of other subjects . Of course his comment will sound good around the old spitoon at the feed store back home.

Then there is Sen Jim Dimwit of South Carolina who is a Pee Party" leader" and the intellectual of that group .During an interview on MSNBC on July 6th pronounced that there was no need for additional income for the US Treasury and that reduction in spending was the answer to balancing the deficit. Stated tax income for the past several years was in excess of previous years A visit to the Politifacts Truthometer will show how this buffoon gets by on the ignorance of his listeners or constituents. Recently he asked Jamie Dimond whose too big to nearly fail bank JPMorgan lost in excess of three billion dollars for financial advise for the US Treasury, AND in a fawning way I can add.

And going back in time, honorable mention to William F. Buckley of the posturing intellect with big words everyone would look up. He "got off" on a tax evasion charge in Republican controlled court.

I briefly encountered him as he sailed his yacht in Connecticut waters from empty slip to empty slip to avoid docking fees. My friend with a sailing yacht with a fireplace no less,told me this piece of gossip as we bid Buckley farewell motoring away from one slip to another in the same marina one foggy day. At that point he had not yet faced the tax court so he had to save on Yachting costs!.

Buckley formed the stodgy "National Review" "to read Dwight Eisenhower out of the conservative movement", we can see how successful he was. – it caters to the nearly dead rich folk of the US. Circulation,150,000. Whoopee!.

Typical conservatives , all the same, hypocritical and artificial except in their own eyes. AND JEB BUSH DOESN'T LIKE THEM EITHER!

AUTHORS OF THE RIGHT ARE WRONG AND SHOULD LOOK UP THE WORD.

And in addition why in the world are they needed.?

They strain to be meaningful like the Prohibitionists of the 1920s when only a few governed the tastes and desires of the many .True there are still "dry counties" or entire towns that by blue law do not have access to alcoholic beverages but they are so far from other areas that do serve liquor retail and wholesale they can never hold sway over meaningful number of residents in an area .

On a business trip a number of years ago I stayed with the owner of a firm in the heart of Tennessee who had to travel to a city 60 miles away for liquor so when he made the trip he spent over a thousand dollars per visit.

This did not stop drinking in the area , just made it more attractive.

Editors of "Right" conjob oriented publications seem to be deluded into thinking they are meaningful to the overall population but their attitude is they do not care if even the Republican party adheres to their obvious ridiculous vision as to what is needed for America and it's citizens. Their advocacy postulates pure "conservative " rule even if they cannot define it.

What make them more laughable is their reach to the reading public. If 10 mIllion people read a newspaper every day they have less subscription than a quarter of a million people per day which is hardly permeating the country -their lifelong aim.

But then self delusion is a trait of the elitist class of publishers who have devoted their lives to a vanishing concept . For instance what is conservative about a nation that has a debt of $ 250,000. Looming over the head of every child born.,a nation that goes to war with the wrong country not even knowing the cost or how to win and lying about the rationale? Actually advertising and promoting war among it's citizens like a soap powder or deodorant?

Question the next "conservative" you talk with. Ask about our deficit and how they define winning a war long since lost.. after the second election of George W.bush, Face it, as of June 2012 a hundred Iraqis can be blown apart at any given time by other Iraqis, look in the newspapers ,our invasion was a self inflicted disaster for us and an invitation for the invaded nation to enter into civil war.

From the U.S. (Us Suckers) standpoint General Petraus and the surge were a façade .After eleven years all that can be said is we are out of there and we left a half billion dollar embassy to do what?

Returning to our "con men" Time magazine with a circulation of over TWENTY FIVE MILLION subscribers allowed the following comments (abridged) by advocates of the party that got us into the mess we now are facing with no conservative solutions other than tax cuts for individuals and corporations that already have them. Financed by having poor and old people starve(cut foodstamps) or die of sicknesses that worsen because Medicaid is discontinued regardless of mortal illness.

Erick Erickson, blogger for RED STATE -Erick feels there is an internecine war going on in his party between RINOS AND THE PEE PARTY which will require a purge from 2012 to 2016. He is willing to lose this election for future purity .Good idea!

Rich Lowry-editor of the mighty 150,000 circulation NATIONAL REVIEW catering to nearly dead wealthy people. Rich(aptly named) feels his so called party is on the verge of "greatness" prepared to overcome the dreaded Obama inspired medical plan led by Robme in a government facsimile to the Reagan regime (president Ron could never join this glut of fanatics and idiots per his own son nor would they have him unless he was dead and stuffed) Lowry seems to purposely overlook the eleven instances when Reagan raised taxes when needed and his BIPARTISANSHIP (STRANGER WORD?) with Democrats when necessary.

Nick Gillespie –Editor of "Reason",also TV version- Nick gets lost in looking for solutions for his cult which he fails at miserably. Feels Obama will be reelected!

Ann Coulter-This skank can't seem to like anyone even previous Presidential candidate McCain .The bitch says there is no crisis in the "party" and all many of them are interested in is getting a gig on FOX "news" which may be true, it is a bench for losing candidates. She thinks the group whoever they are should be more interested in saving the country. Rah Rah! And How? She has no answers,her aim is ink and money.

AND FINALLY THE EFFETE SNOB of NO TAXES EVER,GROVEL NUTTWIST.

I refer of course to Grover Norquist who is paid by the wealthy and super rich to prevent their money from escaping any pursuit that does not profit them.

His theme in TIME is simple,"Could you just leave us alone." Republicans grovel before him because he twists their...., you know.

Almost all GOP Congressmen and Senators have signed his cult pledge like ALCOHOLICS IN NEED OF SUPPORT.They pledge to never increase taxes in their elected position.

This guy is president of AMERICANS FOR TAX REFORM and is a lobbyist who covers the waterfront coercing Republican politicians to sign his pledge against raising taxes in turn promising financial support from many self interested greedy groups with secret money for political use against mainly Democrats who have pledged to serve their constituents rather than a blind Warbucks multi purpose money bank .

When the Democrats or ANY political candidates believe their constituents need a government that requires money for education ,returning soldiers need mental healthcare and paraplegic operations or job training, cities and states need roads and bridges OR the Federal government needs more examiners at the IRS TO APPLY the tax code the Nuttwist pledge should never exist, it is the essence of greedy penurious bastards at the level of governance. And gee, where was it when we invaded Vietnam,Iraq and a number of other locations without a quote on cost?,

So let's outline a perfect example of the ONE PERCENT LEAVING THEIR CLASS ALONE and SUFFERING TO THE TUNE OF BILLIONS FOR IT. You must recall a man APPOINTED BY GEORGE W. BUSH to chair THE S.E.C. ,one of the one percent born to wealth named Christopher Cox. His Grandfather is deceased President Richard M.Nixon,President of the United States . He married a wealthy heiress and was well educated at Harvard Law and elsewhere, Was elected to Congress and served Republican Presidents as well as Democrats in appointed posts.

One of Cox's closest friends was Arthur Laffer, whose famous curve drawn on a napkin made him the phoney godfather of supply-side economics. Laffer staunchly defended Cox against conservatives criticizing his inactivity.

The chairman, said Laffer, "has got a whole staff there that [has] been appointed by previous people." Well, not exactly. Shortly after Cox took office, The Washington Post reported that senior turnover at the commission gave him "an unusual opportunity" to appoint several key lieutenants. Donaldson had already appointed Linda Thomsen to the second most powerful position at the commission, chief of the Division of Enforcement. Would Cox replace her? No. Thomsen stayed. The decision set the tone for Cox's chairmanship. He would strive to avoid controversy. "In his job, it makes no sense for him to be a bull in a china shop," says Laffer.

My previous feelings about Laffer are further reinforced. It was reported during Cox's tenure investigators who wanted to subpoena documents or compel interviews faced cumbersome processes to gain the commission's approval for each case. Enforcement officials had to see the SEC commissioners (plural)before approaching a company about a civil settlement and Cox personally postponed such cases as Bioval eventually weakening the sanctions sought.

Among other oversights Cox enforcement against "naked SHORT SELLING" was sorely missed. Wonder why? according to many former agents interviewed after he was replaced by Susan Shapiro, an Obama appointee.

Allow me now to introduce Bernie Madoff ,former head of the NASDAQ who" made off "with billions of many other one percenter's lucre in the largest PONZI SCHEME ever perpetrated on the US economy. It started in the 1970s and the collapse due to the costliest whistle ever blown was during Chris Cox's term at the SEC in December of 2008,a period of 38 years. As his friend ``W" bush was packing for Texas.

For thirty years Madoff because of his reputation as head of NASDAQ was believed to be a financial genius at profitable trading and was trusted by hundreds of super rich families, among them the owners of the New York Mets baseball team who are even now engaged in litigation involving a loss of over 170 Million dollars they were legally obliged to pay back to other Madoff victims after the Wilpons had taken profits from the Ponzi fund.

While Madoff was reporting thousands of non existant trades numerous whistles blew only excess saliva, one investigation that never happened started at Madoff's firm in Midtown Manhattan and where investigators learned

Madoff personally would be their primary contact. He graciously provided them with contradictory information. But when they sought to confront him about it, he said he had already given the information they wanted to investigators in Washington -- which was news to the SEC officials in New York.

Shortly thereafter, they concluded their investigation without answering the questions that had spurred the review. Was there a Cox Non aggression pact?

In 2005, fraud analyst and onetime Madoff rival Harry Markopolos wrote a detailed letter to the SEC's Boston office warning, "The world's largest hedge fund is a fraud." The Boston office had worked with Markopolos before and found him credible.

Boston sent the letter to the SEC's New York office, where officials viewed Markopolos skeptically and did not understand his reasoning, which was based largely on statistics. Stats was a tough course in college.The team assigned to look into Madoff had little experience reviewing potential Ponzi scheme.

In May 2006, SEC investigators interviewed Madoff, who didn't bring along a lawyer.How cool can one get? When asked how he consistently beat the market, he told the investigators, "Some people feel the market," the report recounts.

Madoff later told the inspector general that he expected to be exposed when he told the investigators that his trading was processed through the Depository Trust Co., an important financial intermediary. He gave the SEC his DTC account number, which they could have used to verify the trades he claimed to have made.

"I thought it was the end, game over. Monday morning they'll call DTC, and this will be over," Madoff told the watchdog earlier this year. "And it never happened."

The report calls the agency's decision to never verify Madoff's trading "the most egregious failure in the Enforcement investigation." That investigation was closed in August 2006. It took a single phone call to DTC after the Ponzi scheme was exposed in December 2008 to find out that he had not placed any trades with his investors' funds.

Concerns about Madoff's firm continued to arrive. In March 2008, the office of then-SEC Chairman Christopher Cox received an e-mail from a source who had contacted the agency several times, urging investigators to look into secret files Madoff maintained on a computer he carried. Cox's aides sent the e-mail to the enforcement division.

An enforcement staffer who had worked on the Madoff case replied: "[W]e will not be pursuing the allegations."

At this point I will make the obvious statement that Madoff 's fund after 9 investigations over 30 years was finally found to be a gigantic fraud , hence December 2008 brought down the house of Madoff.! When the stuff hit the fan Cox said in his statement "The commission received"credible and specific allegations regarding Mr.Madoff's financial wrongdoing" but did not respond aggressively ."NO "bull in a china shop for him! Or Laffable Laffer. After all he was a one percenter making more of them!

AND IN EXCESS OF 60 to 90 BILLION DOLLARS, STILL INCREASING, GONE!

Passing strange, one of the actors on the stage along the way conducting one investigation was Erik Swanson who served as a lawyer for the SEC commission for ten years .He was married to Shanna Madoff in 2007, a niece of Madoff, daughter of his brother Peter who was the firms' compliance officer!

The Dominos and falling cards did not hit her or husband Erik Swanson.

Dominos are so interesting. Surely considering the Consequences the fiscal solitude isolation Grovel Nuttwist seeks for himself and his cult at a cost of over 50 Billion dollars and the thousands of ruined lives of investors'families should not be duplicated or sought by any government official or cloud headed lobbyist cultmaster. OR ANY UNELECTED AMERICAN IDIOT!

The one percenters should remember that taxes are the price we all pay for civilization,those with the most lose most which If it collapses, considering Europe, may be possible.

DESPERATE

The situation in the UNITED STATES OF AMERICA in the year 2012 is as follows for the Republican choice for President of our nation.

The former one term Governor of the state of Massachusetts, Mitt Romney has changed his beliefs on almost all important matters relating to governance of the people of the United States since he started his run for office.Not just in detail,nuance but in total substance.

Romney in the most important matter of National Health Insurance has repudiated the plan that was developed under his direction known as Romneycare that was the basis for the current operative plan adopted by the Congress and found Constitutional by the Supreme Court of the United States now labeled Obamacare by all parties. Including President Obama because he cares. For Americans.

The Romney plan as functioning for seven years in his former state has 90% of the residents pleased with it. People who are affected by the national plan developed under Obama have also been well served by the tenets that prevent insurance companies from disallowing coverage for existing illnesses and coverage for up to 26 year old student members of a family living in the household of insured to be covered by less expensive family medical coverage...the cost of drug plans also have been lowered substantially. And more benefits come in the next 24months.

Romney has chosen as a Vice Presidential running mate Paul Ryan the congressional head of budget committee who espouses 20% tax cuts for the wealthiest people on top of those that already were adopted under previous deficit creating disaster W. Bush He further proudly endorses the change of the cost of coverage   for Medicare age 54 and under and the abolition of Medicaid affecting 18 million working poor,disabled and dependent children and others near poverty many whose very lives depend on the government subsidy as it now exists. This scheme can cause the deaths of hundreds of thousands of innocent citizens of the United States in the next four years. You can hasten their demise by voting the GOP way. (GOP = GAS OLD PEOPLE)

Worse, According to analysis by the non partisan Tax Policy Center Ryan's plan in total will result in 4.3 Trillion IN ADDED DEFICITS OVER TEN YEARS.

Furthermore Ryan has changed his mind on the so called "defense "budgeting. which he and hundreds of other Republican Congressmen endorsed less than two years ago. This Republican budget is 640% higher than that of our purported chief adversary, China.

And since then we have removed our military from Iraq and are now gradually leaving Afghanistan _.But Republican political dollar support is from the Corporations and lobbyists that make military goods of all types. So we have LITTLE FLIPPER and BIG FLIPPER RUNNING FOR OFFICE and their own self seeking positions, not for America's well being and safety..do you think China will attack America? We owe them TWO TRILLION DOLLARS.! And buy billionsof their goods every day.

The Political Campaigns   of Ryan, the undertaker in the cheap suit and   ETCHASKETCH Romney are desperate in the half truths and outright lies they tell and the false tales they have other telling for them, "DOCUMENTARIES TWISTING

"FACTs "beyond belief including their strawmen billionaires financing from behind the curtain like the WIZARD OF OZ who was also an EXPOSED FRAUD. They do all for Koch Bros. and dozens of other WARWHORE or POLLUTION industries that seek to invade Iran on the ground which of course would be another losing proposition like the last two Republican plans of ten year losing MILITARY FIASCOS. The losses were 50,000 casualties,paraplegics, suicides, post traumatic mental illnesses increasing everyday and FIVE TRILLION dollars IN DEFICITS HIDDEN BY OFF BOOKS ACCOUNTING BY W BUSH AND COMPANY.

If the Republican neocons are now considering sending a quarter of a million men into an area that has one and a half billion religious fanatics who hate our country and have no value for their own lives that would be suicide, as is proven daily as we speak. A ground war in Iran would have worse results than we have already seen in the Arab Countries..

The US Conference of Catholic Bishops has recently criticized the Ryan budget for cutting food stamps, medicare, Medicaid and other programs helping the poor who with Ryan's assistance may not be with us very long. His plan does not meet the"moral criteria" per one of their many letters directed to Congress. Not that this writer has any respect for the amoral ejected former Republican House Chairman Newt Gingrich as person or human being but his critique of the Ryan plan as "extreme social engineering" is precise and truthful for a change..Gingrich claims to be Catholic and is a known Republican.

Truth spoken in the heat of primaries is like the saying" in vino veritas". Gingrich and "Ryan are 2 of the sabatoging15 Republicans including Sen. Ensign, Dement and Kyl who met on the eve of Obama's inauguration arranging to obstruct and filibuster every Democratic plan in Congress from day one to regain power in 2012. Slime ball governing.!

So in closing Americans should not give up Medical care, Social security and normal lives for such impossible horrible ventures for the benefit of two percenters   who thrive on other's misfortune and live high in their accumalated greed.. Good luck to all of us in the next election, WE SHOULD ALL HOPE AND PRAY IT'S NOT RIGGED OR PAID FOR.